FIX THE YIPS FOREVER

FIX THE YIPS FOREVER

HANK HANEY

with Matthew Rudy

GOTHAM BOOKS

GOTHAM BOOKS
Published by Penguin Group (USA) Inc.
375 Hudson Street, New York, New York 10014, U.S.A.
Penguin Group (Canada), 90 Eglinton Avenue East, Suite 700, Toronto, Ontario M4P 2Y3, Canada (a division
of Pearson Penguin Canada Inc.); Penguin Books Ltd, 80 Strand, London WC2R 0RL, England; Penguin Ireland,
25 St Stephen's Green, Dublin 2, Ireland (a division of Penguin Books Ltd); Penguin Group (Australia), 250
Camberwell Road, Camberwell, Victoria 3124, Australia (a division of Pearson Australia Group Pty Ltd); Penguin
Books India Pvt Ltd, 11 Community Centre, Panchsheel Park, New Delhi – 110 017, India; Penguin Group (NZ),
cnr Airborne and Rosedale Roads, Albany, Auckland 1310, New Zealand (a division of Pearson New Zealand
Ltd); Penguin Books (South Africa) (Pty) Ltd, 24 Sturdee Avenue, Rosebank, Johannesburg 2196, South Africa

Penguin Books Ltd, Registered Offices: 80 Strand, London WC2R 0RL, England

Published by Gotham Books, a member of Penguin Group (USA) Inc.

First printing, November 2006
10 9 8 7 6 5 4 3 2 1

Gotham Books and the skyscraper logo are trademarks of Penguin Group (USA) Inc.

LIBRARY OF CONGRESS CATALOGING-IN-PUBLICATION DATA
Haney, Hank.
    Fix the yips forever : the first and only guide you need to solve the game's worst curse / Hank Haney with
Matthew Rudy.
        p. cm.
    Includes index.
    ISBN 1-592-40236-4 (hardcover)
        1. Golf. 2. Golf—Training. I. Rudy, Matthew. II. Title.
GV965.H24 2006
796.352'3—dc22   2006024533

Printed in the United States of America
Set in Minion, with Scala Sans and Copperplate Gothic
Designed by BTDNYC

CONTENTS

FOREWORD
by Mark O'Meara

1998 MASTERS AND BRITISH OPEN CHAMPION AND SIXTEEN-TIME WINNER ON THE PGA TOUR

Looking back on the almost twenty-five years that Hank Haney has been my friend and teacher, I can now see just how much he suffered from his problems with the driver yips—and what a good job he did keeping it a secret. I can remember the Spalding program tournament at Pebble Beach in 1985 like it was yesterday. I was playing in a group in front of Hank. The pace of play was pretty slow, so I got a ringside seat for one of the strangest rounds of golf I've ever seen. Hank was spraying tee shots all over the Monterey Peninsula—into the ocean from the sixth tee, and down onto the beach from the ninth tee. He actually played up from the beach on nine and saved par. When it was over, I walked over to him. He looked completely spent. I put my arm around him and asked what the damage was, expecting him to name a big, big number. Instead, he told me he shot 73. It was one of the greatest 73s in the history of golf, but it was also just the start of what turned out to be an almost twenty-year struggle with the driver yips. Nobody called it the "driver yips" then because, honestly, we just didn't understand it. Sure, we all knew guys who had "lost their swings," but it wasn't something you talked about. It was easy to think that it couldn't happen to you if you didn't go fooling around with your swing and make some ill-advised changes—and, honestly, it's still a subject tour players don't like to think about. In reality, the yips are really one of golf's dirty little secrets.

Hank basically gave up playing soon after that, but I thought it was mostly because he didn't have the time to devote to the practice it takes to play well. He was teaching me and a bunch of other tour players, and running a thriving business at his golf ranch outside Dallas. Hank was a big part of my Masters win in 1998, from the work we did on my swing beforehand to the putting advice he gave me tournament week. I invited him to come and play a round with me at Augusta after the win, to celebrate a little bit, but he said he had a scheduling conflict. In Hank's business, being busy is a good thing, so I didn't think twice about it. I mean, how much golf does David Leadbetter or Butch Harmon play? I would soon find out that a full lesson book wasn't the real problem.

I knew something was different in 2003, because I came out to Dallas to work with Hank on my game and the first thing he wanted to do was go play golf at Vaquero, the new club he had joined outside Dallas. We played thirty-six holes, and Hank made a bunch of birdies and broke par in both rounds. I immediately started teasing him about his new pre-shot routine—which is one of his keys for beating his driver yips—and about his new, lower ball flight. "Bud, you can start picking on me when I miss a fairway," he said. And he only missed one, so I didn't have much to say. Better yet, the old Hank I used to play with back in the 1980s was back.

I know how much Hank loves the game, and I know how much he loves to play. So when I heard about the hundreds of hours he had spent by himself up in the second floor video center at the Golf Ranch late at night, hitting balls in front of the camera and trying to figure out why his driver swing was going so wrong, I knew how painful it must have been for him.

He's a perfectionist when it comes to the golf swing, and he didn't want to play in public when he wasn't in control of his game.

Hank went through so much with his own yips problem—and learned so much about the yips themselves in the process—that it was easier for me to listen when he confronted me about my own putting yips late in 2003. My putting stroke had been deteriorating even before I won the Masters and British Open in 1998. In 2003, I had my worst season as a professional and fell out of the top 100 on the money list for the first time in my career. Using the new ultrasound technology he's got at the Golf Ranch, Hank showed me the yip in my stroke, and we worked out a way for me to short-circuit it with my "claw" putting grip. My confidence came back immediately, and I won in Dubai in the spring of 2004. I've always trusted Hank with my swing, with great results. He came through for me again when it came to dealing with my putting yips.

The yips can make you feel like you want to quit golf and take up fishing full time. I know. I've been there. But Hank's experience and sensitivity to the problem make him unique in the world of golf instructors. If you have the yips, you couldn't be in any better hands than Hank Haney's. If you can't make it to McKinney, Texas, for a personal diagnosis, this book is the next best thing. The yips don't have to be a death sentence for your golf game.

GOOD LUCK.

FOREWORD
by Marius Filmalter

If you had told me ten years ago that I would be living in Dallas, conducting research with Hank Haney on the yips and helping hundreds of people recover from this terrible problem, I wouldn't have known what to say.

Ten years ago, I was a teaching professional working outside of Munich, Germany, helping average players to hit the ball a little bit better. Just like every other teacher, I had students who suffered from the yips. And just like a lot of other teachers, the methods I had at my disposal to help these people weren't much more than guesses based on anecdotes I had heard from other teachers and players.

But in 1999, I started teaching a scientist, Dr. Ernst Pöeppel, and we got to talking about perhaps taking a more systematic approach to the yips. We spent four years doing research, trying to determine what *kind* of problem the yips are—physical, psychological, or neurological. And, frankly, we didn't get very far. We realized that if we wanted to make any further progress, we needed to develop a device that could measure the yips. With the help of some engineers, we coinvented a device that could accurately measure the phenomenon—the SuperSAM ultrasound machine. In October 2003, we presented our research and the device at the European Teaching and Coaching Conference in Munich. Hank Haney was the keynote speaker at that conference. That fact would change both of our lives—and, we hope, the lives of thousands of people suffering from the yips.

After we presented our findings at the conference, our booth was very busy, filled with teachers curious about our research and the knowledge of the putting stroke that became available as a result of our research. Hank was one of those teachers who came by. I will never forget that first day of the conference, when Hank, nonchalant and very unassuming, quietly watched our presentation. He did not say much, did not ask much, was just standing in the corner assessing what was happening. I had never met Hank, but fortunately, I was introduced to him on the next day of the seminar by Oliver Heuler, the organizer of the event. From then on we were constantly discussing, exchanging ideas, and philosophizing about the yips.

Hank was—and is—incredibly inquisitive and open-minded about new ideas, characteristics that have certainly contributed to his success as a teacher. He wanted to understand more about this affliction, both because of what he had suffered through with his own driver and because it had the potential to help so many other players.

The long and short of the story was that he, most graciously, invited me to relocate to the United States, to his Golf Ranch in McKinney, Texas. My task was to initiate the most comprehensive research on the yips ever undertaken, and Hank and I would use that research both to help players with the yips and to get a better understanding of the putting stroke and why good putters are so good.

I've been working with Hank outside of Dallas since the beginning of 2004, and it's been the most interesting phase of my career. Not only have we made great strides in understanding just what the yips are and how to help people who suffer from them, but the thousands of players we have measured have given us a tremendous database from which to learn about the putting stroke itself. I've also had the chance to watch and help dozens of tour players, including Tiger Woods and Mark O'Meara, something that would not have been possible without my association with Hank.

We're still at the beginning of this research process, relatively speaking, but the information in this book will do more to advance the cause of curing the yips than anything I've seen. If you have the yips, there is certainly hope that you can enjoy the game again. I'm proud to say I have been a part of the effort to make that possible.

FOREWORD
by Steve Johnson

DIRECTOR, HANK HANEY GOLF RANCH
1998 NORTH TEXAS PGA TEACHER OF THE YEAR

According to the National Golf Foundation, there are more than twenty-seven million golfers in the United States. Of those individuals who identify themselves as golfers, studies have indicated that approximately 26 percent of all golfers have some form of the yips in their game. The high percentage of golfers with the yips is one of the main reasons for the lack of growth in the game of golf. The author of this book, Hank Haney, is a great example of a golfer who left the game he loved for years because of the yips. If the yips can drive one of the best teachers in the world away from the game, more attention must be paid to the diagnosis and cure of this golf pandemic.

Although researchers have been able to figure out that yippers are more likely to be lower handicappers, the yips can affect golfers at any level. Whether your yip is in putting, chipping, pitching, or full shots, it is a huge obstacle to enjoying the game. There's the reality of knowing you can't hit the ball close enough to the hole to make the putt. The frustration of being told by teaching professionals that your problem is all mental and your only remedy is to not try so hard. The desperation of trying a variety of putters, putting strokes, putting grips, hypnosis, breathing techniques, visual imagery, etc., none of which provide you with any long-lasting results.

And your biggest fear: That you may never cure the feeling of your hand spasm when you strike a putt or hit a shot. All these circumstances are enough to drive any golfer to just quit. I know these feelings all too well because I have been a yipper since 1987. I may have had the putting yips long before that, but 1987 was when I realized that there was something terribly wrong with my putting game.

I experienced my worst episode of the yips after I graduated from college and was playing on a mini-tour. I had a recurring nightmare that would perpetuate the fear of my putting yips. The dream went like this: It was a four-foot putt on a crusty, spike-marked green. The hole was cut on a mound with subtle breaks in all directions. No matter where I looked, I couldn't determine which way the ball was going to break. With indecision, I would line up to that putt and try to be committed to a line. As I stood over the putt I would realize that I had misread the line, and I would start the process all over again. Believe it or not, in that dream, I never hit the putt. I just kept lining it up over and over again in my mind until I woke up in a sweat. Hank once asked me what I felt when I yipped a putt. My best explanation was that I felt the fingers in my right hand explode when I hit certain putts. I never knew when it would occur, but I was certain it would happen.

I have worked as a teaching professional with Hank Haney since 1988 and have seen many students experience the same challenges with the yips. The exotic grips used by yippers have helped some to overcome yipping, but really fixing the problem requires a full understanding of what is actually causing the yip. Hank Haney and Marius Filmalter helped me fix my yips by using a systematic approach to diagnose my problem, explain to me what was happening when I yipped, and create a game plan I could follow to help me overcome my problem. The genesis of this book is the many years of experience, observation, and research conducted by Hank and Marius. This book provides all the tools you'll need to fix your yipping problems, along with examples and drills to help you along the way. The great news is that with the help of Hank and Marius, my putting is better than ever. No more nightmares, and no more exploding fingers. I am confident that this book will help you as much as it continues to help me and my students enjoy the game of golf.

INTRODUCTION

The summer of 2002 was supposed to be an exciting time for me. Business had never been better at my teaching ranch outside Dallas, and a course I built—Texarkana Golf Ranch—was opening soon. The course looked so good. You'd think that I couldn't wait to play it. I couldn't wait, but I first had to face something that had wrecked my game for the last twenty years. I could watch you hit ten shots and fix your slice. Some of the best players in the world trusted me to help them with their swings. But when I played, I had no idea where my next tee shot was going. I had the driver yips.

One morning, I went out alone with a carry bag and one of those eighteen packs of cheap balls. I lost every one of them by the time I made the turn. The next day, I tried it again, this time with a friend. On the first tee, I swung my driver and caught it dead flush. And hit it a hundred yards to the right of where I was aiming. My friend yelled, "Come back!" as soon as I hit it. Before it even landed, I said, "Bud, there's no use cheering for those. They aren't coming back."

When people come to me looking for answers to their chipping, putting, or full-swing yips, I know the frustration. I know what it's like to be on the verge of quitting a game you love. Not only do I understand from the perspective of a teacher who has helped people fix all kinds of swing problems for more than twenty-five years, I've been there myself. I played fewer than ten rounds of golf from 1985 to 2002 because of my driver yips. I turned down two separate invitations to play Augusta National, and refused to do any teaching clinics that required me to hit driver. All of this was happening as I was having professional success teaching players like Masters and British Open champion Mark O'Meara. Believe me, I know how frustrating the yips are.

For too long, the yips have been considered one of the game's unsolvable mysteries. Players have spent millions of dollars on new putters, thicker grips for their wedges, hypnotism tapes, self-help books, and psychotherapy to fix the yips. Usually, those fixes are only Band-Aids, if they even help at all. Just look at the professional careers that have been ruined—or at least challenged—by the yips. Johnny Miller and Ben Hogan had the putting yips. Bernhard Langer has made at least four major changes to his putting stroke to fight them. At least two top-50 golf instructors I know have the chipping yips. And I believe the driver yips—not fatigue, stress, or mechanical swing problems—have sabotaged the careers of David Duval, Seve Ballesteros, and Ian Baker-Finch. This clearly isn't something small, rare, and isolated.

Through my own long, painful, twenty-year process of discovery—and with help from a team of European scientists who have studied these kinds of problems in other walks of life—I have found a way to help you find relief from the yips.

Why is that important to you?

Because this problem, in all of its forms, is more common than you think. Using cutting-edge ultrasound equipment, we've taken measurements of the chipping and putting strokes of hundreds of players, from tour level to complete beginner. A quarter of the players we tested had some kind of involuntary yip-like movement in their chipping or putting stroke. Assuming that percentage is in the ballpark for players with full-swing yips, too—and I believe it is—this means that hundreds of thousands of golfers around the world are simply beating their heads against the wall when they take conventional lessons. It's as though they broke a leg and the well-meaning doctor gave them a rabies shot. They'll never get any better until they recognize this problem and treat it the right way.

This book will show you the right way. It will help you discover for yourself if your problem is, in fact, the yips, or some other kind of mechanical swing flaw. If you do have the yips, it will help you diagnose what kind, and how they are affecting your putting, chipping, or full swing. Once we've isolated the problem, the book will provide a series of exercises and drills to iron out the twitches in your stroke. Don't burn the yips into your game forever by practicing the same flawed stroke over and over again. Learn how to short-circuit your yips and swing freely again.

In the month after the *Golf Digest* cover story about my driver yips appeared in August 2004, I received more than 1,500 e-mails from players with a variety of different yips problems. I've done more than thirty instruction articles for *Golf Digest* since 1992 (and only one of them before the yips series showed me hitting a shot with a driver—across an open field, not at a golf course . . .). From those e-mails to the conversations I've had with hundreds of players around the world, I've never had that kind of response before. Players at every level, from the professional to the complete beginner, are crying out for help with this problem. This book is the first real effort to help. You'll see from the letters from players I've worked with at the end of each chapter what an emotional subject this is, and how excited people are to finally be able to do something about it.

1. WHAT ARE THE YIPS?

One of the fascinating things about golf is the way it seems to expose a player's weaknesses. A guy who struggles to hit it straight off the tee ends up having to find a tight fairway on the 18th hole. A tournament might come down to getting up and down from a sketchy lie. A player who's been struggling with his putter has to make a tricky six-footer to get into a playoff.

Because players at every level work so hard either to improve on those weaknesses or disguise them, it isn't any surprise that the yips have been one of the game's dirty little secrets. Nobody wants to talk about a problem that seemingly comes from nowhere and has traditionally been almost impossible to fix. It's easier to watch the other guy struggle with it and turn away, or to make a joke about it later on—while secretly thanking the golf gods that it isn't happening to you. Of course, that works only until it *does* happen to you.

It's safe to say that players have been suffering from the yips for as long as there have been people playing golf. Actually, you don't even have to be a golfer to have the "yips." We're understanding more and more about the motor-function problems that are the root of the yips, and those problems crop up in anything that requires fine motor skills. Basketball players like Shaquille O'Neal get the yips and can't make free throws. Baseball players like Steve Sax get them and can't throw the ball from second base over to first. Concert pianists have their hands seize up during stage performances. Writers lose the feel in their writing hand and can't hold a pen. All of those problems are the "yips," as they've come to be defined.

In golf, players were talking about putting yips as early as the beginning of the last century, even if they didn't really understand what they were or where they came from. "Whiskey fingers" were something players who drank too much (or got old and burned out) suffered with, and they were considered a natural progression for the unfortunate players who had "bad nerves." By the 1940s, the famous teacher Tommy Armour was telling stories about the putting "jitters" that pushed him from playing tournament golf over to the teaching range. The actual term "yips" was first popularized in the 1960s, when Armour used it to describe the tremors in his hands that made it impossible for him to putt.

Throughout the 1960s and 1970s, when golf was first becoming a popular television sport, a variety of prominent players suffered from the yips—even if they were called something else by the media, television commentators, and the players themselves. Ben Hogan was a notorious yipper—to the point that he once proposed that putting be eliminated from the game in favor of a series of nets into which players would have to hit approach shots. Sam Snead's putting yips drove him to try virtually every kind of alternative putting stroke he could dream up. He wound up putting sidesaddle, standing facing the target and to one side of the target line (a technique eventually banned by the USGA).

In the 1970s, Johnny Miller had a streak of some of the hottest golf in the history of the game, routinely winning events by ten or fifteen shots. What most people didn't know was that Miller suffered from the yips to varying degrees ever since a college coach changed his technique. Miller won the

1976 British Open with a serious case of the yips—one he was able to beat only by focusing on a red dot of nail polish painted on the butt end of his putter grip while he made his stroke. When Miller won his last tournament, at Pebble Beach in 1994, he admitted in his press conference that he had yipped every single putt from under ten feet for the week. Tom Watson went from being one of the great clutch short putters in the history of the tour to a guy who needed to hit it really, really close to the hole to win a tournament.

From the 1980s through to today, players haven't become any more willing to talk about the yips than they were before, but they've been willing to experiment with different putter types and strokes in greater numbers than ever before. Two-time Masters champion Bernhard Langer has overcome the yips three different times in his career, first by switching to a stroke that anchored his putter to his left forearm and eventually by switching to a long putter. Vijay Singh won't admit that he's got the yips, but he's been going back and forth between a belly putter and a cross-handed grip for the last few years, and it's been my experience that guys who feel confident with their putter don't switch to alternative grips or longer shafts. He's definitely got a vulnerability there. Chris DiMarco had a horrible case of the putting yips when he was a mini-tour player, and now he's made more than $15 million on the PGA Tour with an alternative putting grip, a version of the claw.

These players are just the ones you hear about, and just the ones with putting yips. Players who get serious cases of the yips tend to disappear—both from the PGA Tour and from recreational golf. Seve Ballesteros still has one of the best short games on the planet. But the last time he played a full season on the European Tour, he led the tour in putting and didn't make a single cut all year because of driver yips. David Duval won the British Open in 2001, and before that shot a 59 on Sunday to win the Bob Hope. Does anybody really think that some kind of mechanical problem like his posture could make it so that he's missing fairways by sixty and seventy yards and struggling to break 75? David Duval didn't forget how to play golf. He's not a bad player, just like Mark O'Meara didn't all of a sudden become a bad putter. He's a good player who has the yips.

Because chipping and driving yips get so much less attention than putting yips, the players who get those forms of the problem don't know what to make of them. They haven't heard of anything besides the putting yips. They try to fix their mechanics—which is impossible—and come up with something to work around the problem, or they quit the game. Jim Hardy played on the tour before becoming a prominent teacher. He quit tournament golf because his putting yips were so bad. And the fact that chipping and full-swing yips are more devastating to a tour-player's score than putting yips—which can be worked around with a grip change—make them even less understood. We admire Chris DiMarco for going to the claw grip, and we watched him take Tiger Woods right to the limit at the Masters in 2005. But when a scratch player gets the full-swing yips, he starts shooting 85 in a heartbeat. I know that better than anyone. When a tour player gets them, he just can't compete. The chipping yips are similar in that they ruin the rest of your game because of all the pressure to be more accurate to make up for it. The only guys you see in professional golf with those kinds of problems are the ones who are brave enough to go out there and keep trying.

At this point, you're probably thinking to yourself, "I've heard of the yips, but what exactly *are* they?" That's a good question, and one we're only now starting to figure out.

Let's start with the basics. A yip is an involuntary movement in the hands or wrists (or both) during a stroke, almost always at impact. When a player's hands twitch like that, the result is usually a jerk or a stab at the ball that produces an inconsistent result. The most familiar form of yips is in putting, but they happen on short-game shots and in the full swing as well. I know all about the full-swing yips, and I know how they can wreck your game. I had them for almost twenty years.

For a long time, the conventional wisdom was that the yips were an emotional or psychological problem. They supposedly had something to do with stress, or with choking under pressure. Players who developed that familiar twitch at impact were suffering from the yips because they didn't have the nerves to putt anymore. I suppose that makes sense intuitively. After all, tournament golf is all about pressure, and performing a complicated task under that pressure. It makes sense that players could make some kind of stress-induced mistake in those situations.

Except that there's one major problem with that theory. If the yips are a psychological problem, why haven't psychologists been able to cure them? Why haven't players been able to go and get some confidence from sessions with a psychologist and get back to a smooth putting stroke? My friend Mark O'Meara saw three different sports psychologists about his putting, but he never got any better until he accepted the idea he had the yips and changed to the saw grip. His fix came when he made a change to a different kind of grip, not because of a psychological breakthrough.

There's another school of thought that the yips happen because of some kind of mechanical flaw. A player yips a putt or a chip because he has a bad grip, or a problem with his takeaway or some other identifiable mechanical issue. I don't completely disagree with that theory—as you'll see in the third chapter, mechanical problems can make you *think* you have the yips, and they can be a precursor to the yips, but I don't think this theory explains the problem fully. After all, we've measured hundreds of players with the yips who have an otherwise mechanically sound stroke.

Probably the most prominent study of the yips is one conducted by a team sponsored by the Mayo Clinic. That team came up with a theory that the yips are a combination of a neurological problem called focal dystonia and performance anxiety. Focal dystonia is a neurological problem characterized by the loss of motor control of the muscles. It happens to people who have to stay in some kind of specific position—like concert pianists or guitarists—for a long period of time. It usually happens in the fingers and wrists, and the simple way to describe it is that the "wiring" that connects different muscles in the fingers and wrists to the brain gets confused. The brain wants to fire a certain muscle, but the signal gets crossed and it either fires a different muscle or the correct muscle, but too much or out of sequence.

The Mayo Clinic sorted the group of players they tested with a survey, basically, asking players if they had the yips before testing the ones who said they did. Then they measured what kind of muscle and brain activity was happening just before and during impact. I think that's too late.

What makes me think I know? It starts with a meeting I had with a team of German researchers in Munich in 2003.

I was invited to go to Germany in the fall of that year to give a talk at the European Teaching and Coaching Conference. I was in the middle of figuring out my own problem with the driver yips, so I was fascinated to meet and talk to a group of researchers who had been doing their own study on the yips. The group was made up of Dr. Christian Marquard and Dr. Ernst Pöeppel, who did the clinical and medical research, and golf instructor Marius Filmalter, who handled the golf side of the project.

They wanted to approach the problem of the yips from a different angle, and they started by devising a way to measure exactly what a yip was, and when it happened in a putting stroke. Now, this isn't as easy as it sounds. You can take the worst yipper of all time and ask him to describe what's happening to him, and he'll be able to give you the play-by-play. Usually, it's something like "I feel like I lose all feeling in my hands when I get to impact, and I just have this spasm." But how do you compare one kind of yip to another? Is there such a thing as a mild yip and a severe yip? Do the spasms happen in both hands? One hand or another? When, exactly, do they happen in the stroke? Is it just at impact, or is it happening way before that?

No matter how perceptive you are, it's impossible to answer those questions with any detail if you're talking about your own stroke. The research team decided that the best way to start to seriously study the yips was to devise a machine that could measure putting strokes and show, both graphically and with number values, exactly what was going on with both a normal stroke and one that was affected by the yips. What we're doing here is defining the problem. Once you do that, you can figure out the best way to fix it.

The machine they came up with is one of the most fascinating things I've seen in almost thirty years of teaching. It uses sound waves to constantly measure where the putter is in space during a stroke. It can tell us where you're aiming at address, what the putter is doing on the backswing, the through swing, at impact, and at the finish. It tells us how long your stroke took, and how consistent the timing of your backstroke and through swing are from one stroke to another. It can tell us if the face of the putter is open or closed at impact, and what the path of your stroke looks like—whether it's straight back and straight through, or moving on some kind of arc.

The machine, which is called the SuperSAM, is cool because it accomplishes two major things. It gives us a frame of reference for what a "yip" is—when it happens, how big or small it is, and what it does to putting performance. It also lets us build a graphic representation of what a great putting stroke looks like. After measuring almost 3,000 players on the machine, we can say with complete confidence that good putters have a certain menu of things they do really, really well. Even if you don't have the yips, knowing that information can help you make more putts.

Over the last three years, Marius Filmalter has refined the machine and moved to Dallas with it to measure more players at my golf ranch. He's now got almost 50,000 strokes in his database, which gives us a pretty good foundation to start to describe what the yips are, when they happen—and most importantly for the people who have the yips, how to fix them.

Here are some of the things we've learned over that time. Let me qualify this by saying that we can come to some conclusions based on the data we've collected, but this is still uncharted territory. We don't have a clear idea of why or how the yips start in one player instead of another, or why a specific kind of drill or treatment works with one player's yips but not another's. But by identifying the problem, when and where it happens, and *how* a certain player responds to the different drills we've devised, we have had a tremendous success rate fixing the yips.

First, there are two different kinds of yips: directional and acceleration. Directional yips come from the hands and wrists trying to overcontrol the alignment of the clubface through impact. Acceleration yips come from the hands and wrists applying a burst of speed through impact. You see both kinds of yips in putting. Good players with the yips almost always have the directional kind, because they seem to have more awareness of where the putter is through the stroke. Beginners or poor players usually suffer from the acceleration type of yips, probably because they still try to help the ball with the hands instead of letting the stroke provide the power. Chipping yips are almost always the acceleration yip type, for that same reason. The player is subconsciously concerned about getting the ball airborne, so he makes a scoop move at impact. Full-swing yips are nearly always the directional variety—trying to overcontrol the clubface at impact, which restricts it from releasing.

The yip itself is an uncontrolled movement of the hand or wrist during the stroke, but it isn't like the other kinds of tremors that you see in medicine. Generally speaking, you see two kinds of hand tremors in people who have them from some kind of medical condition. Either the tremor is present and then goes away when the hand is called on to perform some kind of activity, or the tremor isn't there until you try to use the hand to do something. A yip is neither one of those. When you get the yips, what you have is a neurological misfire. It's a tremor that doesn't happen at any other time except when you perform a *specific* motion with the hands and wrists.

If you're a right-handed player, you're most likely to get the yips in your right hand, but you can get it in the left only, or even both hands. The opposite is true for left-handers. A yip in the right hand (for a right-handed player) causes the most disruption in the stroke, because the right hand has a leading role. This is why a modified putting grip is the most common way for players to address a "standard" case of the yips. Switching to left-hand low or some other alternative grip puts the right hand in a passive position and gets the left hand to take the active role.

In the nearly 50,000 strokes we've measured, we've never seen a yip happen in the backswing. They all happen from the time the putter (or wedge or driver) starts the downswing, down through impact. *When* the yip happens in that time span can vary. You can have an early yip, which starts right after the top of the backswing, or a medium or late yip. An early yip happens 150 milliseconds before impact, while a late yip happens right as the club hits the ball. And just as there's an early, medium, and late yip, we also classify the "size" of the yip, either light, medium, or heavy. A player with a light yip can usually figure out a way to work around it. It might happen only occasionally, and in a way that doesn't have a severe impact on results. But the light yips almost always deteriorate into more serious problems. A mid-level yipper will always experience the yip in his stroke, and would probably feel it in both putting and chipping. Heavy yips are the kind that make people quit the game. They're always present, and a person basically can't putt or chip with that kind of tremor.

We've also found that virtually no player (we're talking three out of more than 3,000 that we've measured) yips during a practice stroke.

In the course of doing this research, we've measured more than 3,000 players. The numbers don't lie. More than a quarter of those players we measured—and it's a mix of tour players, good amateurs, average golfers, and beginners—have some form of the yips. The people we measured weren't just players who were coming for help with the yips or with other putting problems. We measured random tour players at tournaments in the

United States and Europe. We measured average golfers at courses around the country. The cross section of players represented in our database is wide. The Mayo Clinic study estimates that 33 to 48 percent of all serious golfers have experienced the yips. Even if we're conservative about how we characterize the yips and the people who have this problem, there are still millions of golfers who are suffering. Most of them don't know what their problem is, and they might quit the game not knowing. That's something we want to fix.

I said earlier that I don't believe that the yips are a psychological problem. That's true, but they can certainly cause some psychological issues in a player's game. Tour players are the most susceptible to this, since they're making their living at the game. If a player has a slight case of the yips, he can make it less severe by practicing a lot at playing around it. That means trying some different putting grips, or using a low-lofted club to hit running chips instead of high ones. And it's really true that when you see a player grinding a lot around the practice green, hitting lots of chip shots, you can almost guarantee that he's got the yips, and he's looking for a way to work around it.

But one of the fascinating aspects of this problem is that a low-level yipper can be functional by practicing a lot, but he can't ever get rid of the problem that way. It's only when you address the yip directly with drills or technique changes that you can get a lot better. In that sense, it's almost better for a player with a low-level yip problem not to know about it. If he thinks he's doing okay, that's probably healthier psychologically than experiencing the anxiety of *knowing* you've got the problem. But if you address it directly, you can definitely get better.

One thing we want to do is differentiate the yips from the other problems a player can have with his stroke. When you talk about putting, a player can have the yips, or it can be something less dramatic. A player could have bad mechanics. He could be setting up with his body out of alignment, which puts him in position where he has to cut across the ball to hit it at his target. That cutting-across move feels a lot like a yip. If you're set up with your eye line wrong—something we'll be talking about in Chapter 3—you're going to have trouble seeing the line and hitting it where you're aiming with any kind of consistency.

A player could also be missing putts because he's choking. It happens every week, at every level of the game. A player is standing over a five-footer that could win him his first PGA Tour event (and the $900,000 prize), and he just goes into brain lock and pushes the putt badly. That isn't the yips. That's a guy choking because of the pressure. I'm sure you've felt the same thing in a game with your friends. The stakes aren't as high—but they only have to be high relative to your normal comfort level. If I showed up and asked you to play a $500 nassau, you might be worried if your regular game was for $5 or $10. You'd be nervous even if you were fairly confident you could beat me. It's just outside your comfort level.

Other researchers have come to some interesting conclusions about stress and what it does to putting performance. Dr. Debbie Crews, who is a part of the team the Mayo Clinic put together for its yips study, measured how players' emotions changed when they were putting for money prizes, as opposed to hitting putts with nothing on the line. The players who did well had the same emotional reactions as the ones who struggled, but their emotional response was spread out over both hemispheres of the brain. The players who struggled tended to have the response in just the left side of the brain. Her conclusion was that players could improve their putting by keeping the right side of the brain engaged, with things like visualization. I don't disagree with that conclusion. It's just important to figure out if nerves are the reason you're missing putts, as opposed to having the yips.

The simplest explanation of them all is that sometimes you just don't putt well. Of all the strokes we've measured, Tiger Woods has the best one—the best in terms of being the most consistent or the most repeatable. His results obviously speak for themselves. But he goes through stretches where he isn't making them. It's a mixture of mechanics and confidence, and that's true for every player. But if we can peel away the mechanical problems and address the confidence and choking issues, that should leave a solid putting stroke. If there's a yip in there, that's fine. We'll get to work and fix it.

2. RECOVERING FROM THE YIPS: SUCCESS STORIES

You probably had the same reaction to hearing all that historical information about the yips as I did when I put it together. There's really no other way to describe it than discouraging. So many players have struggled with this problem—and struggled in secret a lot of the time—that it's easy to think you might be better off quitting golf.

But you don't have to quit.

The purpose of this chapter is to show you that the yips aren't hopeless. They aren't a death sentence for your golf game. I made it through them, and I'm playing as well as I ever have. I went from losing a sleeve of golf balls every hole to going thirty rounds without losing a ball off the tee.

What you'll find in these stories, about everyone from Mark O'Meara to the average player from a club like yours, is that recovering from the yips is a process. It starts with recognizing that you've got the yips. It has its ups and downs—times when you think you aren't ever going to hit another ball without a yip—and, eventually, you have a breakthrough. Trust me. You can enjoy the game again. It's too much fun to miss out on.

CONFRONTING—AND BEATING—MY DRIVER YIPS

What do you do when you make your living helping people understand what they're supposed to do with the golf swing, but you can't figure out why you're hitting your own drives into places where you can't find them?

And when I say I couldn't find the tee shots I was hitting starting in the early 1980s, I really mean it. By the time the driver yips had completely taken over, I couldn't predict within eighty yards where my tee shots would go. I'd get to impact and the face of the driver would open, and I'd catch it flush, but hit it completely off the property. Or, I'd try to control the face and keep it from opening and hit it 290 yards—but a hundred yards off-line to the left.

What the driver yips did was keep me from playing golf for almost twenty years.

I'd love to be able to tell you a dramatic story about the first time I had the driver yips, and how I knew what kind of trouble I was in for. But it didn't happen like that. If anything, they kind of snuck up on me during a time when I wasn't playing much golf. I can remember feeling like something wasn't quite right during a few rounds I played in high school, but I thought the answer was to just practice more.

When I got to college, I was always pretty wild with the driver. I even tried to play with a super-low-compression ball, because I knew my chipping and putting were good and I figured that if I could just find my tee shots, I'd be okay. If it didn't go too far, then it couldn't go too far off-line. I wasn't going to challenge for a spot on the PGA Tour when I graduated from Tulsa in 1977, but I was a pretty good college player—good enough to make all-conference. I knew teaching was what I wanted to go into when I got out, so I started by taking jobs working under prominent teachers Jim Hardy and John Jacobs, before making it to Pinehurst, where I became director of instruction.

I started to have problems with my driver in the early 1980s, when I was beginning to spend a lot more time on other players' games than I did on my own. Mark O'Meara and I were working together a lot after the 1982 season, and I had a full schedule of lessons and golf schools, first at Pinehurst and then at PGA West and Stonebridge Country Club outside Dallas. Since I didn't have the time to practice my own game as much as I wanted, I didn't expect as much from myself when I did play competitively in PGA section events. I'd have rounds where I had no idea where the driver was going to go, but I attributed that more to rust than any other problem.

But as time went on, those rounds where I had no feel for the driver became more and more frequent. I started backing out of outings that required me to play, and I got pretty nervous about demonstrating the driver for students during lessons. Mark told you in his foreword about the incident that really was the final straw for me, at Pebble Beach in 1985. He's not exaggerating that story at all. I was really looking forward to the trip out to California with Mark, but I was nervous about putting my game on display. Mark was in the group behind me, and Craig Stadler was in the group ahead. I spent the entire morning the day of the first round on the range, trying to figure out some kind of punch swing that would let me get around without embarrassing myself.

I don't know if you're familiar with the course map at Pebble, but it's pretty hard to hit it in the ocean off the tee on the sixth hole. I hit my tee shot 150 yards off-line, into the water. I hit it in the ocean again on the ninth hole, but saved par from the beach before pull-hooking my tee shot on 10 and hitting it out-of-bounds off the tee on 14. I was literally shaking from exhaustion when I putted out for my all-world 73 on the 18th hole. I took twenty-one putts to do it, and the experience pretty much finished me when it came to competitive golf.

I came back to Texas and basically put my clubs away. All because of the driver yips. I almost completely stopped doing clinics that required me to hit drivers in front of people. The only way I could do it if I absolutely had to was to look back at the crowd while I hit shots. I'm sure that seemed like some kind of neat trick shot to those audiences, but it was literally the only way I could hit those shots.

My relationship with *Golf Digest* started in 1992, when I joined the staff as a *Golf Digest* teaching professional. From 1992 to 2004, when I first told the story of my driver yips, I did more than thirty stories for the magazine. Only one of those stories—a 2001 cover story about fixing a slice—showed me hitting a driver. I probably set the record for consecutive stories about ball-striking with your irons.

It was obvious to me that there was something really wrong with my driver swing. I mean, it's my job to be able to watch your ball flight and understand what things you need to improve in your swing to get better as a player. I've spent my whole career developing my ability to do that. From the beginning, I was in front of the video system in my studio, studying my swing frame by frame and trying to figure out what I could do mechanically to make this problem go away.

I spent years this way, watching swing after swing on video. It was so frustrating, because my swing looked great—except for the moment of impact. What I know now is that my drive to fix the problem—hitting hundreds of balls—just made the yips worse. The yips are a motor-skill problem. Your brain knows what you want to do. The signals just aren't getting through to the muscles. Doing it over and over again just makes that problem worse. You can't do the same things you always did. You have to create a new pathway in the brain to perform the movements you've always made in a different way.

I never had any success with sports psychologists, so I didn't go that route. I didn't know anything about the yips, or motor-sensory problems. So I started trying to make my swing "perfect." It was a disaster. I was out there teaching a 20-handicapper who hit a thirty-yard slice, but he could go out there and find his ball and enjoy himself. In February 2003, it dawned on me that if I was ever going to play again, I had to stop trying to hit perfect shots with a perfect swing and just try not to yip when I hit it. And that was the start. The first piece toward solving the puzzle.

My goal changed from trying to make a perfect swing to trying to make a swing that didn't have a yip in it. If I could make a yip-free swing, even if it was an ugly one, I could go back and fix the mechanical problems later. I started where a lot of people with the putting yips start—by changing my grip to something that reduced as much wrist and hand movement as possible. I've always taught a traditional grip, so the one I ended up using is pretty extreme. It looks like something taught in Moe Norman's "Natural Golf" method. I moved the handle from my fingers to a more diagonal position in my palms.

The new grip worked the way I expected—I had almost no hand or wrist action. I hit a dozen balls that way, and you've never seen somebody so happy to hit some ugly, low, weak shots to the right. I didn't yip one.

Once I made the grip change, I worked on my swing just as I would anybody else's. I made a few setup changes to try to get the ball up a little bit more. I wanted to stop thinking about the same things that caused the yips before, so I completely changed my pre-shot routine. I wanted my mind to be completely clear, so my new routine barely looks like a golf swing at all. I take the club almost straight up in the air on the backswing, and I turn and look at it. I'm focusing on getting my clubhead, arms, and shaft in a good position, and forgetting about the ball and the target. Then, I make a downswing way above the ball—almost like a baseball swing. I used to tilt my head down to the right through impact. Now, I make a conscious effort to tilt it left in both my pre-shot routine and real swing.

With the yips, the real frustration comes when you make a nice practice swing without the flinch, and then yip it on the real swing. I wanted to keep the same, relaxed feel I had developed in my new practice swing when I was hitting a real shot. Essentially, I wanted to forget about the ball. So I started focusing on the brim of my hat during the downswing. After I take my backswing, I basically don't look at the ball again until I walk up to it on the fairway.

It took fifteen years of searching, but I finally found the secret to beating my driver yips. I'm hitting straighter now than I ever have.

With this new grip, new pre-shot routine, and new visual drill, I went out and started to play in early fall 2003. I didn't yip it. My ball flight was lower than it used to be, and I had to relearn how to "play" again. I was making stupid mistakes—pulling the wrong club, taking too many chances. But those were mistakes I could work on. I love the game, and I was able to play again without embarrassing myself. A month in, I made three birdies in a row, and my game was really starting to come around. I joined a new club in Dallas—Vaquero—and started playing almost every day. I played thirty rounds between October 2003 and February 2004, and my handicap index was plus 2. I played thirty-six holes with Mark O'Meara, and I missed one fairway. I made seven birdies in a round and shot 66. I play better now than I ever dreamed I could. It's been twenty-five years since I shot scores like that. It's great to be able to play like that, but more than anything, it's a feeling of relief. Did I find my old swing again? No. I found something new. But it works.

RANDY SMITH AND THE CHIPPING YIPS

Randy Smith has been an institution in Dallas since before I got here in the early 1980s. The head professional at Royal Oaks Country Club, he's gotten some national attention for teaching players like Justin Leonard, Harrison Frazar, Hunter Mahan, and D.A. Weibring, and for winning the PGA's National Teacher of the Year award in 2002, but Randy is probably more proud of the fact that more than fifty of the junior players he's taught have gone on to get college golf scholarships.

I knew Randy by reputation when I first moved to Dallas, but the first chance I got to spend any time with him was when my playing partner and

I were paired with Randy and his partner at a North Texas PGA section event. We played the first few holes, and I was just amazed at how Randy hit the ball. He was long off the tee and hit his irons just great. He was two or three under when the story got a little clearer. On a short par-4, he just bombed a tee shot down there, fifteen yards short of the green. He proceeded to blade that chip over the green, then stub the next two from the back of the green. He had some of the worst chipping yips I've ever seen—and it was just tragic to watch because of how good his long game was.

We kept in touch sporadically over the years, but both of us have busy schedules. It wasn't until I was putting together the story of my own driver yips for the August 2004 issue of *Golf Digest* that we reconnected and talked about his problem. He had quite a story to tell.

Randy can remember the day his chipping yips started—after a casual round at Tulsa Country Club in 1975. After muffing a couple of chips, he decided to go to the range and work on his short game before he went home for the night. He spent four hours there, yipping one chip after another. He told me he's never played a round of golf since without feeling a yip in his chipping stroke.

His short game—and overall confidence—continued to deteriorate, and he hit bottom in 1985 at another North Texas section event. Standing over a fifteen-yard chip shot, he yipped the grip of his wedge so violently that it kicked backward into one of the pleats of his pants, ripping them wide open. By the time Randy went to Scotland the week before the 2000 British Open for a golf trip with Justin Leonard, he had given up using his wedges. He spent the whole trip putting from as much as fifty yards off the green. You can get away with that in Scotland (and in a lot of Texas), but it's tough to play the game—or teach the short game—when you can't hit those shots.

In just the few months before Randy and I got together at my golf ranch in the summer of 2004, he had tried more than fifty different chipping methods to quiet his yips—everything from a variety of contorted grips to a home-made, super-heavy wedge. The guys at *Golf Digest* got the idea to expand the story about my driver yips into a series about the chipping and putting yips. Randy heard about it and came over to see some of the work I had done, both on my own yips and on the problems other players were having. We spent three hours up in the studio, working on the diagnostic machine I have here and going through some drills designed to get him less focused on impact.

For Randy, just learning where the yip was happening in his chipping stroke was a big step. Some players yip in the backstroke. Some yip on the downswing, and others experience the yip right at impact. Randy's yip was coming right at impact, and by trying some drills (which I'll show you in detail in chapters 6 and 10) that got him paying attention to where the club finished in his swing instead of where it was at impact, he made some real progress. He didn't completely cure his yips in that one session—after thirty years, it was certainly going to take more time than one afternoon—but he went home with a way not only to manage them, but to go out and play without embarrassing himself.

When you've experienced the feeling of powerlessness that comes with the yips like Randy has (and I have), it definitely influences the way you teach. I know that my own yips problem made me realize that a lot of the people out there struggling with the game—either putting, chipping, or making a full swing—are going home from a lesson thinking they must not be doing what their teacher asks because they aren't getting any better. In reality, a lot of them are struggling because of the yips, not because they can't learn or don't have the aptitude to play this game.

Understanding that you've got this problem is a big, big step. Randy always knew he did, but learning that he could do something about it took a tremendous amount of pressure off him. He made a really great point about the yips that afternoon. He called the ability to treat the yips one of the most effective grow-the-game initiatives he could think of. We know that people who get frustrated and continue to struggle with the game eventually quit. That's happening at the casual level, with people who decide not to play the five or ten rounds a year they otherwise would, but it's also happening at the club level. Randy's seen it at Royal Oaks. Dedicated players who love the game are leaving it because the yips cause them so much stress and aggravation. Randy saw that there was some hope for those players—for players like him—and that inspired him as a teacher. He wants to keep those players at his club and help them love playing the game again. I know how he feels, because that's exactly what happened to me. I have always loved teaching golf. But when I had the driver yips, I didn't love playing it. Now I love playing it more than I ever did.

MARK O'MEARA AND THE PUTTING YIPS

It isn't an exaggeration to say that Mark O'Meara has been one of the great putters on the PGA Tour over the last twenty years, both in terms of putting statistics and making big putts at important times. It's hard to win two majors and fourteen other tournaments on the PGA Tour (and $14 million in career prize money) without being able to roll your ball pretty well.

I've seen him do it almost from the beginning. Mark and I have worked together—and have been close friends—since 1982, when we met at Pinehurst. Mark was playing in the PGA Tour event they used to have there, and I was working as an assistant pro at the resort, teaching in the golf schools. He asked me if I'd have a look at his swing. I've been doing that ever since.

Mark and I had been through enough together for me to know that something serious was bothering him after his first round at the 1998 Masters. We met on the practice putting green after he signed for his 74, and it was the most down I've seen him in all the years we've been working together. I was trying to encourage him, telling him that he wasn't out of the tournament yet and that everything would be okay. "How can I be okay?" he asked me. "I have the yips from two feet in. I literally cannot make a putt."

At that point, it didn't matter if Mark had the yips or not. You can't expect to play at Augusta National—home to the slickest, most unforgiving greens tour players see during the season—without feeling confident with your putter. It got worse when I watched him hit some putts. He definitely had a yip in his putting stroke. The yip wasn't something we were going to fix right there on the practice green on Thursday night, but I had to give him something to at least get through Friday.

The research we've done over the last few years has helped us understand that alignment problems can cause the yips. Your brain knows you aren't aligned at the target, so it sends signals to the hands to yank the ball back on target. I didn't know that at the time, but I could see Mark had his eyes aligned right of the target, which was forcing him to compensate with his stroke, yanking it back to the left. I helped him get lined up better, so that he could make a compensation-free stroke, and that really seemed to help calm the yip down. He didn't feel completely recovered with his putter, but he hit it good enough to shoot 70 and make the cut comfortably.

On the weekend, he really played well, shooting 68 on Saturday to get into contention. Everybody remembers what happened on Sunday: Mark birdied three of the last four holes—including an eight-footer on 17 and then the bomb on 18—to win by one over David Duval and Fred Couples and earn his first major championship.

How did Mark win the Masters with the yips? It's like getting that feeling in the back of your throat right before a cold hits you. You know you're getting sick. It's just a matter of time before it knocks you out. The yips were in his putting stroke. He obviously managed them very well, even winning another major at the British Open later that same summer. But over the next few years, they became more and more noticeable, and it was clear he was going to have to do something about them.

By 2003, Mark had gone from being one of the best putters on tour to one of the worst. He dropped out of the top 100 in the putting stats and, for the first time in his career, he fell out of the top 125 on the tour's money list. By the end of that season, the yip in his putting stroke had gotten to the point where I could see it on television. I'm sure everybody was paying attention to what Annika Sorenstam was doing against the guys in The Skins Game in November, but I could see from my living room how much Mark was struggling with his yips there.

I met up with Mark in December at the Father/Son Challenge in Florida, where I was caddying for him and his son. I had just come back from speaking at the teaching summit in Germany, where I met the team that had designed a portable machine that uses ultrasound to diagnose the yips. The German teaching pro who was a part of that project, Marius Filmalter, had told me about some of the alternative grips he was teaching to players who were suffering from the yips, and he would later come to Dallas to teach at my golf ranch.

With that conversation still in my head, I talked to Mark about his yips. After the struggles he'd had with his putter in 2003, he was at least willing to consider trying something different. We went out to the practice green early in the week and started experimenting with one grip in particular, called the "saw," where Mark's right hand sat on top of the grip, with the palm perpendicular to the target line.

He was definitely nervous about trying something unconventional like that. "What are people going to say if I go out there with a grip like that?" he asked me. The issue wasn't so much whether it would work or not—he started making putts right away with the new stroke, so he knew it was going to help him. He had to overcome the looks he was going to get from other players when he brought that grip out onto the practice green at a real tournament. It was also about having the confidence to try something different from the technique that was good enough to win fourteen tournaments and two major championships. Tour players don't take those kinds of things lightly.

It also didn't hurt that Vijay Singh was playing in the Father/Son that week, too, coming off a year when he won four tournaments and $7.5 million dollars with his own unconventional putting setup—a belly putter with a cross-handed grip. Mark tried the saw grip for a practice round and didn't yip a single putt. He's putted that way ever since.

It was incredible to watch the transformation in Mark's overall game just from that change in his putting grip. It took so much pressure off his long game, because he wasn't worried about the three- and four-footers you have to make to be competitive on the PGA Tour. All throughout the time he struggled with the yips, well-meaning friends had been telling him the problem was in his head. But he worked with three different sports psychologists, and the problem never got any better. With this mechanical change to his grip, the problem was solved. He knew he didn't have to have a perfect ball-striking week just to make a cut.

It didn't take long for Mark to come all the way back. The next March, he took the saw grip with him to Dubai and beat a field that included Tiger Woods and Ernie Els—his first win on any tour since 1998.

AVERAGE PLAYERS' SUCCESS STORIES

Since the summer of 2004, I've had a putting studio set up on the second floor of my golf ranch in McKinney. It has one of the SuperSAM ultrasound diagnostic machines invented by the German research team I met in 2003. One of the guys on that team, Marius Filmalter, is a talented instructor in his own right. He came to Dallas in 2004 to continue his research and help players suffering from the yips.

We've seen hundreds of players here since then, and with the help of the SuperSAM machine and the drills I'll tell you about later in this book, there have been some remarkable success stories.

Randy Gillespie, a 10-handicapper from Dallas, Texas, had the putting yips for more than twenty years before he came to see us last year. He was regularly four-putting from six feet, and had worked his way through dozens of putters in the year before he came out to the ranch. Randy even came with what we now know are some of the standard sad stories of a player with the yips. When he played in a scramble, his partners would have him putt last, not because he was the "anchor" who could be relied on to make the clutch putt, but because they didn't want to get distracted by his painful yip stroke. Other friends stopped playing with him completely because they felt so bad for him after watching him struggle.

On his first visit to the ranch, Marius had him making strokes left-handed, with the back edge of his right-handed putter. He made three in a row, all without a yip. The major breakthrough was in his setup. We discovered that he was aligned a foot too far to the left on a six-footer. Basically, he had to push a putt for it to have any chance to go in. When he made a "solid" stroke, he thought he was pulling it, because the ball went right where he was aiming—a foot left of the hole.

Once Randy improved his alignment and got less fixated on impact by trying the left-handed putting drill, his yips started to disappear. Now, he thinks about that old feeling of pulling his putts and makes a beautiful, relaxed stroke.

Rick Rappaport, a 4-handicapper from Portland, Oregon, came to us with an even more serious problem. Not only did Rick have the chipping yips, but he had yipped putts, tennis forehands, and even ping-pong shots in his athletic career.

Marius started Rick with a simple chipping drill. Instead of chipping with a sand wedge, he gave Rick a 6-iron and asked him to make chips with his left arm tight against his body. He initiated the chip with some body turn, and concentrated on making a metronomic swing—the same length back and through. Instead of thinking about impact, his goal was simply to turn through the ball and face his target at the finish.

After that simple change, Rick spent an afternoon chipping bucket after bucket of balls. Marius kept telling him that if he could hit one without a yip, there was no reason he couldn't hit two or three or four in a row. At one point, he hit thirty in a row without a yip. Rick struggled when he took it out to the course, but slowly his chipping started to come around. After a month of practice, he virtually eliminated the yips from his chipping stroke.

A LETTER FROM A PLAYER WITH THE YIPS

When you have a passion for something in life, the hardest thing is to watch its quality slowly dissipate, especially when you have done everything in your power to try to stop the slide.

For me I believe it started approximately in the summer of 2000. Walking up to a straight two-foot putt I had one thought in mind. Just take your birdie and savor the moment. Why not? I'd done it enough times before. From two feet this is a "no-brainer." I went through my usual routine of confirming my line, making a few practice strokes and then lining up and pulling the trigger. What happened next was really inconceivable. Not only did I miss the hole by a good four inches on the left, but I had a three-footer for the comeback. What had I just done? Was it a lapse of concentration? Was I distracted? I couldn't figure it out. What I do know is that for the next putt I couldn't find that inner peace to feel I was going to make it. I was really bothered by the fact that I had just missed a two-footer for birdie and was now faced with a *three-footer* for par. Two putts later, I was in the hole. Bogey from a two-foot, slam-dunk birdie putt. Welcome to the world of the yips!

Throughout the years I have played golf, I typically have felt comfortable putting on greens that aren't too undulant, or had a decent surface condition. Two putts were pretty common once I'd hit the green. If I was within ten feet of the cup, birdies were a distinct possibility (not that I always made them, mind you). That summer my "relative" putting prowess was waning fast. Within the next four to six rounds, I had lost all confidence in putting. I could "yip" that ball in any direction except into the hole. Worst of all, the harder I fought it, the worse it got. What I didn't know was that the worst was yet to come.

From that time to the end of the 2004 golf season, my putting average went from about thirty-four per round to as high as forty-five per round. Talk about soul-destroying. I would have days where I couldn't miss the fairway or the green, only to have forty-two or forty-four putts on the day. (Ever have a five-putt? I have. . . .) The next time out it reversed itself, but I never got below thirty-eight putts a round. Boy, did my handicap balloon.

Come November 2004, the cavalry had arrived. (Sans the white steed—this is a good thing, because I didn't need any more manure on the greens.) This was when I met Marius Filmalter. I had heard about his putting instruction and had in fact Googled his name for some background. In a matter of a few sessions with him and his device, I had a reverse claw grip, a renewed confidence, and an understanding of what a decent putting stroke looked and felt like. I was back to being a player again. (We won't talk about the rest of my game, though.) Was it that simple, or was it a "flash in the pan"? Well, as the saying goes, "The proof of the pudding is in the eating." I kept track of every game I played in 2005 and counted every putt. The result: forty-four rounds with an average of 32.56

putts per round. That includes three rounds under thirty putts per round (one with twenty-eight and two with twenty-nine).

Does the product work? Are you kidding me? I'm enjoying golf again with a renewed passion and can't wait for my next round. Obviously I want to score well, but even when I don't, I count my putts and can still walk off the course with a smile. Thanks, Marius. I owe you big time.

JOEL ZEGER
Thornhill, ON, Canada

3. DIAGNOSING THE PUTTING YIPS

How many times have you played a round of golf with your buddies and somebody missed a short putt that meant something in the match? It happens all the time, and I'm sure you've heard the jokes about missing them because of the yips.

Everybody misses short putts—even tour players. But when you start to miss them consistently, it's natural that you start to develop some doubt. Are the misses happening because of some kind of mechanical flaw in your putting stroke? Is it because of nerves? Pressure? Or, as hard as it is to admit it, is it happening because of the yips?

None of those answers is out of line, of course. And that's where I come in—helping you differentiate between a mechanical flaw, a problem dealing with pressure, or the yips. As scary as the yips sound, if we can diagnose them as your problem, we can do some simple and practical things to get rid of them. Just knowing the yips are the problem—and not a bad stroke—takes the pressure off a lot of players I see.

So how do we make that diagnosis? It's actually not much different than what we'd do if we were working on your full swing in a regular lesson. Ball flight is the foundation of how I teach full swing. If you're hitting your 5-iron and the ball is going high, weak, and right, I can understand a few things about what's happening at impact without even looking at your swing. The ball flight tells the story, and so does what I see with your mechanics.

I want to see what you're doing with your stroke. First, I'll look at what the ball is doing when you hit a putt. We'll set up on the practice green for a straight fifteen-foot putt. The goal is to take out outside factors like reading break, so I can focus just on your stroke, not on the decision-making part of your putting game. Then you'll hit a series of five or six putts. How is your speed control? Are you hitting one way past, and then leaving one short? What about direction? Are you missing consistently left or right? What about direction relative to where you're aiming? What is your impact condition? Are you hitting it square on the face, high or low, or toward the toe or heel? Are you hitting it on the upswing or the downswing? Sometimes you can actually see the flinch at impact.

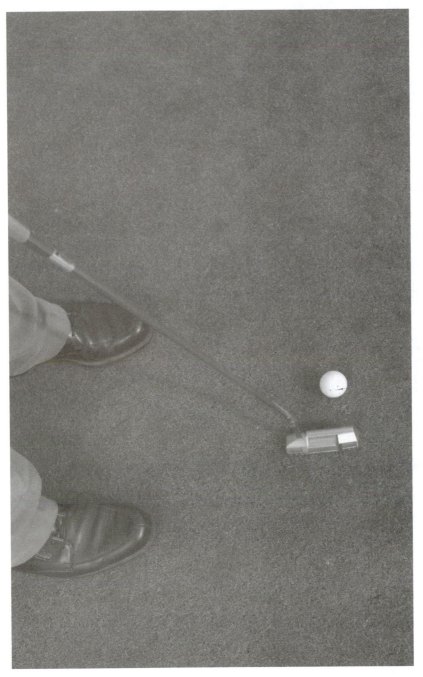

An inconsistent setup position makes it difficult to hit the ball consistently on the center of the putter face. When you strike the ball off the toe, like I am here, the ball causes the putter to deflect off center. The putt will then roll off-line to the right of the target, and it won't roll as far as it should.

Your mechanics are next on my list. How is your posture? Are you slumped or upright? Comfortable or stiff? How is your weight distribution across your feet from left to right, and from toe to heel? Ball position tells me a lot about where your putts will go, too. If your ball position drifts too far forward, you're going to have a tendency to pull putts to the left. Do that enough times and your stroke will change to compensate for it—meaning you'll start shoving the putter open to push the ball to the right.

What does your stroke path look like—is it straight back and straight through, or does it move on an arc? Those two kinds of strokes each have their own set of mechanics that have to match up. If you're trying to make a stroke that doesn't match your fundamentals, you'll struggle. You also have to match your putter to both your body and the kind of stroke you use. A putter with a shaft that's too long will push you into a too-upright setup position. One that's too short will cause you to slump your shoulders and bend forward too much. How the putterhead is weighted also has a big impact on how you hit your putts. If you swing the putterhead on an arc, you need a putter that is built with a degree of "toe hang." That means if you were to balance the putter on your finger, the toe of the putter would hang toward the ground. If you use a straight-back-and-straight-through stroke, you're better off using a putter that's face-balanced. That means, when you balance it on your finger, the face points straight up in the air.

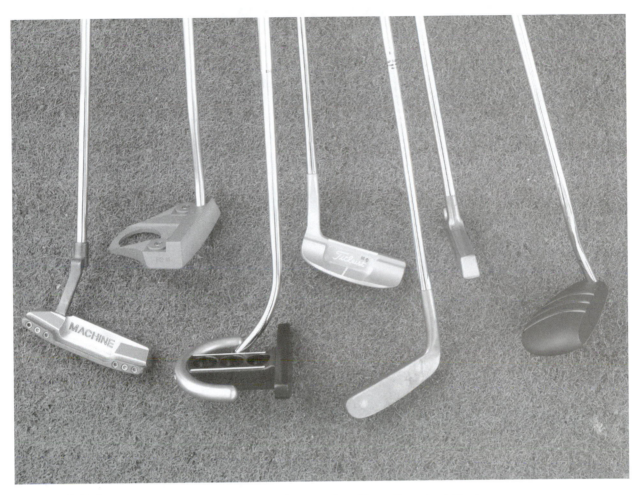

Putters come in all shapes and sizes, but keep in mind that you need the characteristics of the putter to match up with your body and what's going on in your stroke.

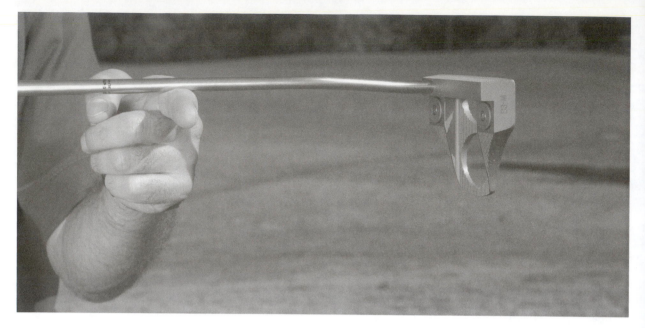

In a face-balanced putter, the face of the club points up at the sky when you balance it on your finger. This putter was designed to work straight up and down the target line, not on an arc.

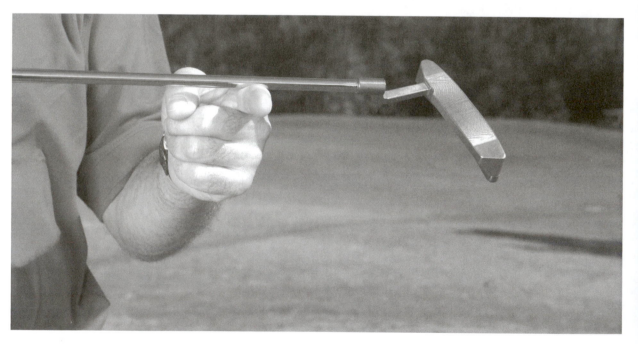

This putter has moderate toe hang. The weighting toward the toe end of the putterhead helps it swing along an arc.

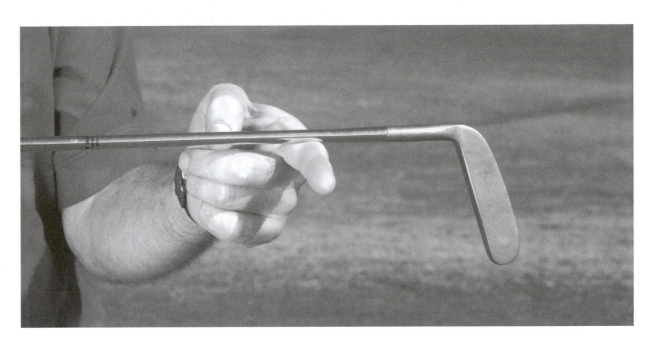

This putter has extreme toe hang. A heel-shafted model like this promotes a full release of the putterhead through impact.

The grip is a critical element to pay attention to. Are you using a conventional putting grip, or something else? If you're using the same grip you'd use to hit the rest of your clubs, that's a quick fix. If you're putting cross-handed or using some other kind of unconventional grip, I'll feel pretty confident about pegging you for a yipper right away. When you look at tour players, anyone who has moved away from a conventional putting grip to either a longer putter or a different kind of grip has done it to relieve some kind of yip problem.

Before we start talking about the signs of the yips, we should go over some basic putting fundamentals, to give you an idea of what to check for first.

The most important elements are grip, alignment, and posture. There are some variations in there, but for the most part, you need to accomplish these things: Have your hands on the putter in a way that lets it move through impact consistently; aim where you actually want the ball to go; and set up to the ball in a way that lets your stroke work smoothly and without a lot of compensations.

The putting grip is different from the grip you use for a regular shot in a couple of significant ways. In a standard grip for a full shot, the club is down in the fingers so you can get speed when your wrists unhinge through impact. In a putting grip, the club runs more vertically, in line with your forearms, and in the fingertips, for more feel. When you set your grip, you want your hands to work together as a unit, and you need to have them set up so that you're aligned square to where you want the ball to go. That means your palms need to directly oppose each other on the grip, and the right palm (for a right-hander) needs to be perpendicular to the target line. It basically represents where the face of the putter is.

In a standard putting grip the hands link together in a reverse overlap grip. Instead of the pinkie finger on the right hand sitting on top and between the first two knuckles of the left hand, as it would in a normal overlap grip on a full swing, the index finger on the left hand sits on top of the pinkie finger of the right. That configuration gives your hands more stability on the club. I've also seen players extend the left index finger so that it runs along the top of the fingers of the right hand.

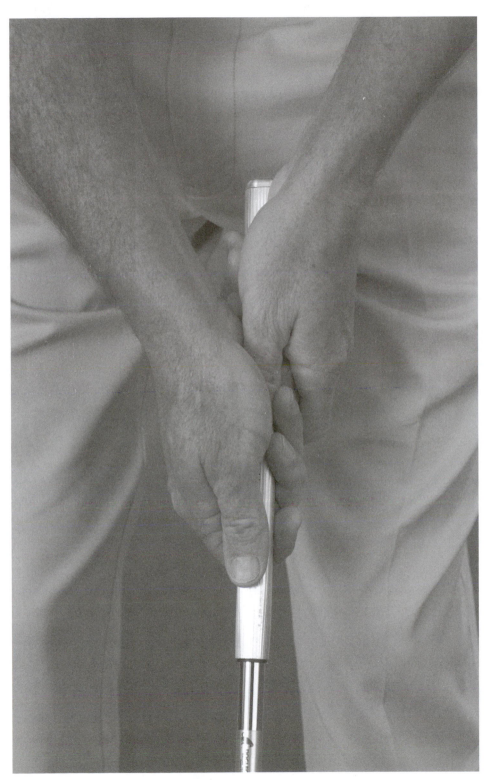

My hands are in good position on the putter here. My palms are directly opposed to each other, and my thumbs are running straight down the top edge of the shaft.

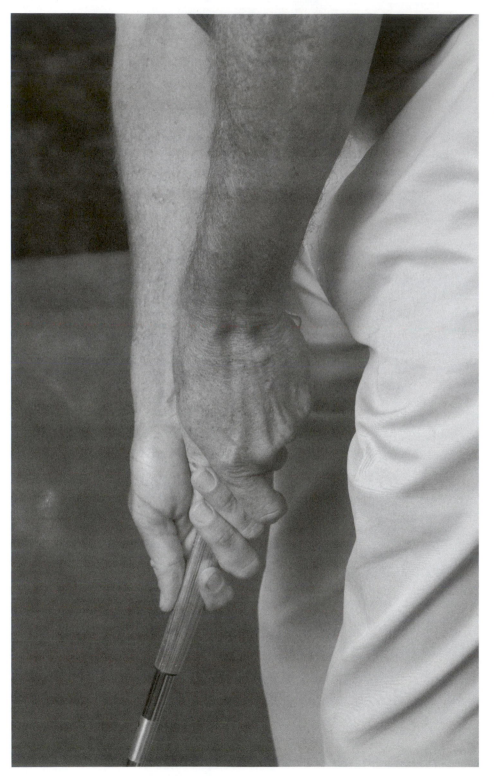

In a standard, reverse-overlap putting grip, the index finger on my left hand sits over the little finger on my right hand.

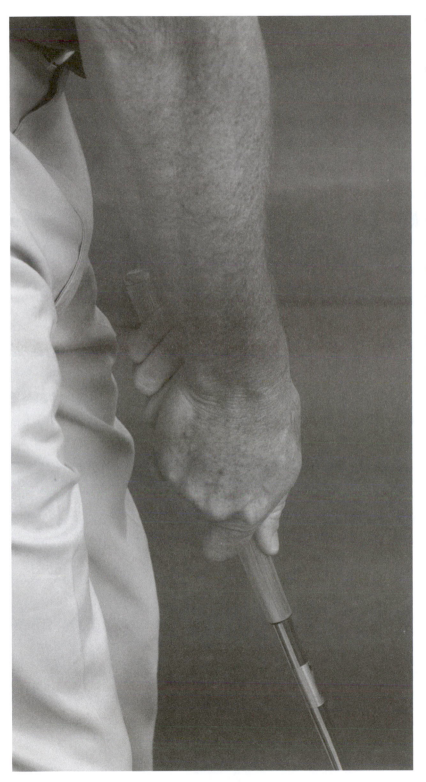

You can see two important things here. First, my arms are aligned—you can't see my left arm peeking out from under or over my right. Second, you can see how the grip of the putter is set low, closer to my body. I'm not lifting the grip up and away.

There isn't any hard-and-fast rule about a putting grip besides the fact that you need the hands to work together and aim you accurately. If you're more comfortable using a regular overlapping grip, go ahead and try it. The goal is to make sure you have maximum feel in your hands. Putting is all about small movements and touch, not strength and bracing yourself for impact. You're looking for a soft, relaxed feel, not a death grip. I realize that's not always easy to do, especially if you think you have the yips. But gripping the club down in the palm or with too much force isn't going to give you more stability—or, for a player with the yips, keep the twitches from happening. In fact, the opposite is true. If you get a tight, restrictive grip on the putter, you're actually *more* likely to lose control of the club, either through a mechanical problem like a bad release or the yips themselves.

One of the big issues I see with a lot of players who struggle with the yips is a grip in which the hands have drifted away from each other. Essentially, both palms are angling upward, not toward each other and perpendicular to the target line. When the hands move that way, it changes the angle that the wrists hinge on. All of a sudden, you've allowed all kinds of play in the wrists and hands. The putter wants to flare open at impact, which is the kiss of death. When the wrists break down like that, struggling to hit your putts in the middle of the putter face is the least of your problems. That grip often leads to the full-blown yips. One of the common threads among players I've seen with the putting yips is that the right wrist gets into an arched position. It happens most often from a bad grip like the one I just described, but it can also come from trying to push the ball out to the right (consciously or unconsciously) with the stroke. We're trying to get you as far away from that as possible.

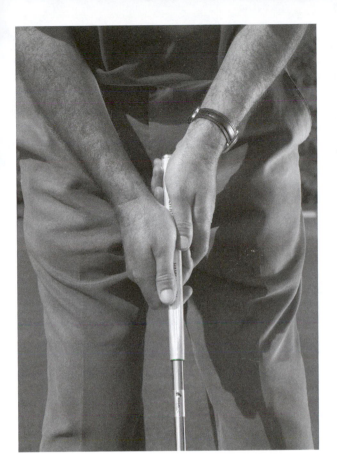 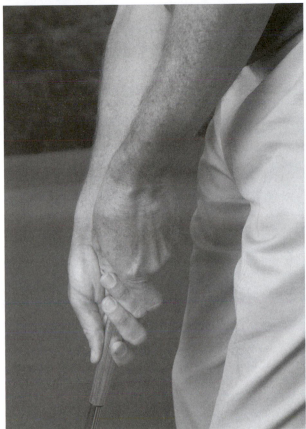

This grip doesn't look dramatically different from a good one, but it will cause you problems. My right hand has turned weaker, or more toward the ground, while my left hand has done the same thing. My thumbs, meanwhile, have shifted from the middle of the top edge of the grip to the edges of the grip. The hands don't work together from this grip.

Compare this grip to the one on page 48, shot from the same angle. That bow in my left wrist is the kiss of death in putting. Almost every player with the yips has a bow in the wrist like that. It brings all kinds of bad wrist hinge into play.

You can hold onto the club the right way (and make a great stroke), but if you can't line yourself up to hit the ball where you want it to go, you're going to struggle. The two key components of alignment are your eye line and the consistency of your body alignment at a few important positions.

Let's start with eye line. When you putt (or hit any shot, for that matter), your swing path will follow the line your eyes are on. In other words, if your head is tilted so that your left eye is closer to the target line than your right, your path will follow to the inside of the target line on the way back and outside on the way through. If you tilt your head the other way, so that your right eye is closer to the target line, your swing path will go outside and cut across the ball on the way through. Taking the putter back to the outside is one of the major, major indicators of a yip stroke. You want your eye line to run parallel to the target line, so that you can make your stroke without any compensation.

Ideally, your eyes should be perpendicular to the ground, in line with and just inside the target line.

I f your eye line gets out of whack, it's very difficult to see the line of your putt properly.

W hen one eye gets closer to the target line than the other, it will influence the line on which you make your stroke. From this position, your tendency will be to pull across the putt and miss it left.

The next step is to get the rest of your body aligned with your eyes. In an ideal putting setup, your shoulders, hips, and feet are all aligned parallel to the target line. That way, your body is working in concert to send the ball where you're aiming it. When those alignments are changed—for example, when you line up with your feet open to the target line, but your shoulders square—you have to fight just to make a consistent stroke. I'm not saying you can't be a good putter from an open stance. Jack Nicklaus set up a little bit open to the target line, and he had a pretty good career. Problems start to creep in, though, when you start aligning too far left (almost no right-handed player I've seen aligns dramatically right of the hole). It creates a situation where you have to push the ball to the right with your stroke to start it on the right line. Again, that's a move that's consistent with players who struggle with the yips.

I n a good putting stance, my weight is centered over my feet—not on
my toes or heels—and I'm not leaning toward or away from the target. It's a very stable platform.

M y arms are hanging naturally from my chest—there's no stretch-
ing toward the ball, and they're not cramped too close to my
body.

I f you drew lines across my forearms, shoulders, hips, and feet, they'd all be parallel with each other and parallel with the target line.

My toe line hasn't changed, but look how my forearms and shoulders are out of alignment. You'll either pull it from here, or instinctively react to the potential pull and shove the putter open and push it.

My shoulders are closed to the target line here. This is a common position for players with the yips to get into. The face of the putter is basically forced to stay open through impact for the putt to have any chance to start on line.

The third element in checking your basic putting mechanics is posture. In general, you want to be set up over the ball with a tilt from your hips, not slumped from the shoulders. By tilting instead of slumping, you give your arms and shoulders room to work smoothly through the stroke, without any interference. I also like your weight to be distributed evenly across your feet and across your stance. Two of the most common faults I see in the putting setup—whether the player has the yips or not—are having too much weight forward, on the front foot, or the opposite, too much weight on the back foot. If you set up with your weight shifted toward the target, it encourages you to take the putter back outside the target line—a symptom virtually every yipper has in common.

If you have your weight shifted back, away from the target, it encourages you to add loft to the putter through impact. Instead of the shaft of the putter being at ninety degrees through impact, it leans backward, away from the target. You can't make solid contact that way, flipping your hands at the ball.

In a good putting posture, you're tilting from the hips, and your back stays pretty straight. Be sure to keep some athletic knee flex. You want to feel loose, not stiff.

When you slump forward in your putting posture, you can't see the line as well, and your arms and shoulders are hindered from swinging freely.

Another critical part of posture is having your weight centered over your feet from toe to heel. You want the eye line we talked about a few pages ago to run parallel to the target line and just inside it. If your weight drifts out too far onto your toes, your eyes will get out over the ball too far. The opposite is true if your weight is back on your heels. Your posture will probably be too upright, and your eyes will be too far inside the ball to see the line accurately.

One of the most common problems I see in putting setups is the tendency to shift the weight too far forward, toward the target. It gives you a false sense of stability.

You might have heard that putting is mostly about feel, and that as long as you are comfortable over the ball, you can putt well. I agree that you want to feel good over your putts, but the reason I pay so much attention to setup is that it has to match your stroke for you to putt well. And if it doesn't match up, you're also more susceptible to the yips.

Just like your full swing, your putter swing moves on a path back and through impact. You can divide the paths most players try to use with the putter into two general categories—straight back and straight through, or on an arc. In a straight-back-and-straight-through stroke, the putterhead stays on the target line (and the face stays square to that line) all the way back through the backswing and all the way through the downswing. In an arcing stroke, the putter moves inside the target line on the backswing, then inside again just after impact.

Regardless of which kind of stroke you use, the feel you're looking for is that the putter is working with gravity. You make a backswing, and the putter is essentially falling down and through the ball, with minimal help from your hands and wrists. The more you interfere with gravity—which is just about the most reliable thing I can think of—the more you drift into yips territory.

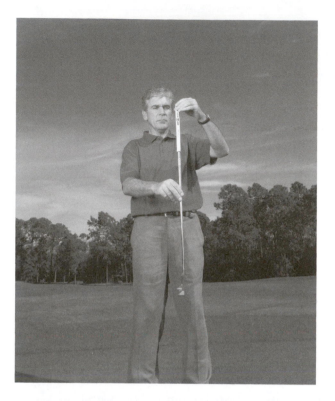

Gravity is the most reliable force you can use in your putting. Let gravity provide most of the momentum, and avoid using your muscles to offset it. Notice how the putterhead naturally opens and closes with no effort.

I prefer a putting stroke that arcs, but there are teachers and players who swear the putter should go straight back and straight through. Tiger Woods, Ben Crenshaw, and Brad Faxon swing the putter on an arc. Loren Roberts has made a lot of money swinging straight back and straight through. Still, the research we've done on players with the yips shows that virtually all of them have used that straight-back-and-straight-through stroke. I believe it's because in that kind of stroke, the putter has to close in relation to the path in the backswing, and then open on the through-swing. The main symptom of directional yips, we're now understanding, is overcontrolling the clubhead and trying to keep it from closing through impact. Take that for what it's worth, but you can see how a stroke that gets you pushing the face of the putter open through impact could lead to problems.

No matter what type of stroke you use, you do have to match your setup to it. If I'm watching you putt, and you're using a straight-back-and-straight-through stroke, you need to have your hands set up higher, away from your body, and your elbows need to be extended from your sides. It's the only way to get the putter to consistently move along the target line. If you have your hands set low and your elbows next to your sides, the only way you're going to be able to hit the ball is to tilt your shoulders and shove your hands at the ball. It's just not consistent.

For an arcing stroke, the elbows sit closer to the body, which promotes a path that moves around rather than straight.

If you use a straight-back-and-straight-through stroke, you need to extend your elbows away from the body to keep the club moving along the target line with a minimum number of compensations.

If I'm watching you swing your putter on an arc, you need a setup that allows for more rotation in the clubhead. That means the hands set lower and closer to the body, the arms softer, and the elbows resting lightly at your sides. As I've said before, if you have a disconnect between what your setup dictates and what your stroke does, you're at best going to struggle to putt consistently well. At worst, you're going to get the yips.

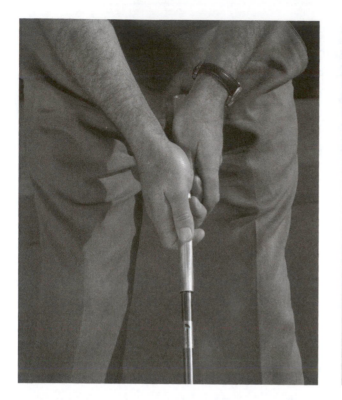

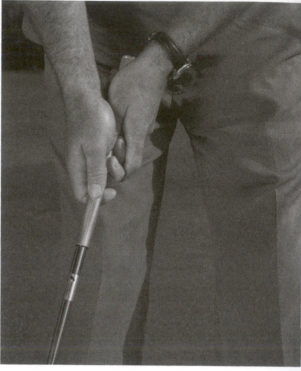

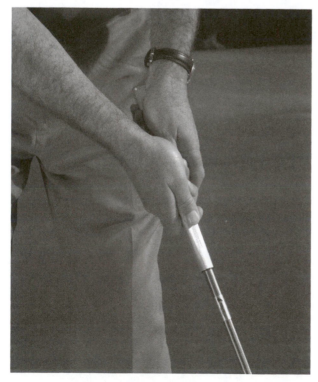

Here you really can see how little the wrists do in a good putting stroke. The force in the putt comes from the entire triangle of your arms and the putter moving back along the arc and then returning to the ball intact, without any "hit" in the stroke.

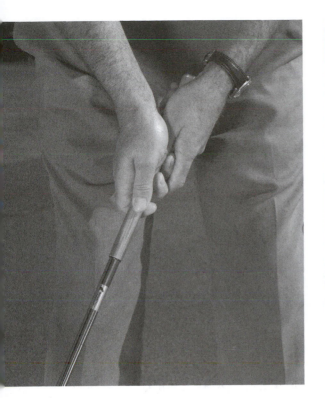
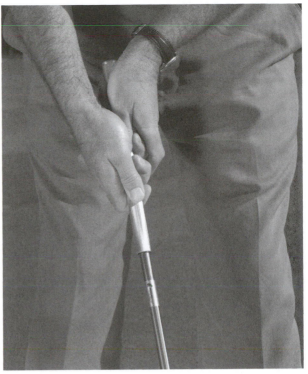

When you compare this photo sequence with the detailed photos of a good putting stroke on the previous page, the first picture in each set looks pretty similar. It's what happens next that throws the stroke off. Instead of swinging the arms through impact, this sequence shows the hands flipping—a common fault. The left wrist breaks down at impact and folds completely on the follow-through. Basically, the right hand has completely taken over the stroke.

Notice how the putterhead follows the arc and appears to open slightly on the backswing. It also stays relatively close to the ground. The shoulders turn slightly back, and then turn through impact. The putter continues to release through impact, and the toe turns upward at the finish.

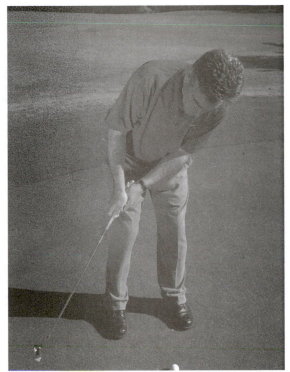

Contrast this stroke with the one you see in the photos on the previous page. Instead of turning, the shoulders rock up and down to keep the putter running along the target line. You can see how the putterhead closes on the backswing, and then opens through impact. Some good tour players have succeeded with this method, but that finish position looks a lot like what a yipper would feel.

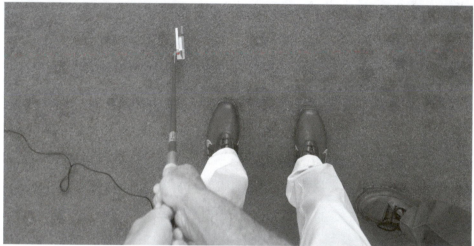

ere you can really see the way my putter moves on an arc—
even on a relatively short putt. The putter moves just inside the
target line on the backswing, then back on the target line at impact,
and then inside the target line again on the follow-through.

Closing the face of the putter on the backswing is a recipe for disaster. You then have to manipulate it open with the hands to hit the putt on-line—a yip precursor.

When you take the putter outside the target line like this, you're forced to make a compensation on your through-stroke. That compensation usually comes in the form of an open putterface—a precursor to the yips.

When a player has the yips, he usually finishes his stroke with the face of the putter forced open, like this.

If we were working together at the Golf Ranch here in McKinney, I'd watch you hit fifteen or twenty putts to try to sort out your mechanical issues, then connect you to a handheld version of the ultrasound machine I mentioned in the last chapter. The TOMI machine uses sound waves to measure the consistency of your putting stroke, and where exactly the putter is traveling in space. Essentially, it gives me a computerized read-out of what your stroke "looks" like—the path it moves on the backswing and through-swing, how the face is moving when you hit the ball, and how consistent you are with the stroke from putt to putt. If you've got the yips, I'll probably be able to see it—and you'll be able to feel it—but the machine confirms it. If there is any doubt, I use a simple test that has proven to be a pretty reliable indicator. I'll ask you to set up with your feet aimed way right of the hole, and your goal is to pull the ball as hard as you can to the left with your putting stroke to get it back on line. If you have the yips, you can't physically do it. I can get you aimed left of the line and you'll be able to push the ball to the right, but a person with a yip stroke can't get himself to hook the ball like that.

If you have the yips, you won't be able to do this test. Set up with your feet pointed way to the right of a hole ten feet away. Now try to hook a putt back to the hole from your open stance. Can you do it? Oh, yeah—a yipper will be able to aim way left and push the ball back to the right.

So what happens if your problem isn't mechanical? What happens if you have a good grip and a solid stroke, but you're missing short putts—usually to the right? You've probably got the yips. Trust me when I tell you that you'll know the feeling. When I had them with my driver, it was as if, right at impact, I lost the sense of where the clubhead was. The muscles in my wrists tightened, and it felt like I wasn't in control of the club anymore. When I talked to Mark O'Meara about his putting yips, he had a similar story. His yips weren't very bad, but even the little twitch he had—a twitch that made him feel like his wrists were just a little bit unstable at impact—invaded his psyche and crushed his confidence.

It's interesting to talk to people who end up having the yips, because you can really see some common themes in the stories. When you start to get into it, the players who have a significant yip will tell you that it really wasn't a surprise when the yips first showed up. Marius tells a great story about a surgeon he was teaching in Germany. She had one of the all-time worst cases of the yips he had ever seen. You would think that the yips—even in a putting stroke—would be a concern for somebody who has a person's life in her hands at her job, hands that need to be stable to work properly. Marius asked her how she kept the scalpel stable during surgery, and she showed him how she turned it around in her hand, almost like a pencil. So Marius switched her putting grip to mimic the grip she used on the scalpel and the putting yips went away immediately.

That story is pretty consistent with others I've heard. A player gets a tremor in his hand if he holds his coffee cup a certain way. Another player gets the yips in a reactive sport like table tennis and just can't return the ball. It's almost a given that the yips will show up for both of those types of players.

If the diagnosis *is* the yips for you, we've got to figure a few things out about it. If you're a right-handed player, your yip is most likely happening in your right hand (and vice versa for left-handers). That seems to happen because the right hand is the hand that controls the clubface in a regular putting stroke. The left hand works more to control the path. The size of the yip has a lot to do with what happens next in terms of treating it. The next step is to figure out the volume of yip you have—light, medium, or heavy—and when the yip is happening in your stroke. Some players have a tremor very early in the downswing, while others feel it right before or at impact. A tremor right at impact indicates that you're anticipating contact. A yip earlier in the downstroke is more of a putterhead control issue.

Once we know those things, we can start to experiment with some drills to get you thinking about different things when you putt. That's a matter of trial and error—each person responds to a different kind of treatment. Which drill or thought process will work for you? Go through the menu of options in Chapter 4 and find the ones that work best. We've had a lot of success with each of them.

How long does it take to fix the yips, you ask? Well, it depends. I know that isn't the most satisfying answer, but the cure depends on the level of yips a player has, how motivated he is to fix them, and how responsive he is to the drills we've devised. The shortest time we've seen is two or three hours, from diagnosis to cure. One of the most prominent amateur yippers in America, Bob Jensen, has been on *60 Minutes* because of his putting yips. He came to the studio last year, and after two hours of practicing some of the drills you'll see in the next chapter, he hit forty-three putts in a row without a yip. He yipped one after that, but then went on another run of good putts. He's not completely cured, but he's putting much better, and he knows he can go out there and putt without yips. Now it's a matter of healing the scar tissue that comes from years and years of damaged confidence.

You do have to be mentally strong to believe that you can putt without a yip—even if you've figured out the way to do it through drills and practice. For some people, it takes weeks or months. Beating them on a consistent basis will definitely take time.

4. ERASING THE YIPS FROM YOUR PUTTING STROKE

You can divide the players who come to the Golf Ranch into two categories. We have players who come to see us because they know they have the yips and they're looking for something to take care of that problem. Other players struggle with putting, but they aren't quite sure why. They think it might be a mechanical issue, or maybe something to do with a lack of confidence.

Each group has its own positives and negatives when it comes to treating the yips. The players who come in knowing they have the yips are motivated. They're willing to try anything to get the problem to go away, because they've had such a long, frustrating experience. The downside is that a player coming in knowing he has the yips usually has a more severe case and usually has more "scar tissue" built up about the yips. And when I say scar tissue, I mean all of the emotional baggage that comes with being a yips sufferer. I know. I've been there myself. You can get to the point where you're skeptical that any kind of treatment will work for you, and that isn't the right attitude to have.

When we "surprise" players with the information that they do, in fact, have the yips, the reactions are fascinating. Some players don't want to believe it. The word "yips" is so loaded with mystery and, honestly, fear that they just don't want to hear it. So they go out and do the absolute worst thing you can do when you have the yips. They grip the grip tighter and hit

500 practice putts to make it go away. Knowing about the problem can almost make it worse because of the psychology that goes with it. Other players hear the diagnosis and let out a huge sigh of relief. It's almost like going to the doctor for a nagging problem and finding you've got a broken bone. It hurts, but it's not the end of the world, and it can be fixed. For players who have the yips but don't know it, it's as if they've been trying to play golf with a broken arm while getting treatment for a sprained ankle. It just adds another layer of frustration on top of the ones that are already there. Finally knowing what the problem is can be incredibly liberating.

Where you fit on that spectrum will influence how you use the drills and exercises you're going to learn about in this chapter. (You can see all the drills I'm talking about, in full color, in the photo insert following page 110.) I'd like to be able to tell you that there's a chart you can scroll down with your finger to find your own particular problem and which solution will work for it. It isn't quite that simple. You're going to find with your own yips treatment that trial and error works the best. I don't have any doubt that within this group of exercises lies the answer for you. You're just going to have to do a little experimenting to get to it.

One thing I will say before I start describing these drills to you is that you might find some of them a little strange. Without naming any names, I went through the complete menu of the drills listed here with a tour player who was suffering from a mild case of the yips. By the time we had some squishy cat toys out to hit putts with, he was looking at me as if I were insane. But by the end of the day, his putting had gotten dramatically better. We put him on the ultrasound machine to compare his yips from when he came in to when he left, and it was like looking at two different players. So suspend your judgment for a little while and try these drills, even if the idea of putting a racquetball around the practice green at your club makes you feel a little bit funny. Trust me. It's worth it in the end.

Let's start with some of the basic exercises we use for anybody with the yips—regardless of how light or severe they are. The goal for all of these drills is to find out what kinds of solutions each individual is most responsive to, and what combinations of exercises start to provide some relief.

As I've said before, virtually no player we've ever tested has the yips on a practice stroke. The research suggests two reasons for this. First, a player isn't anticipating impact on a practice stroke. He isn't preparing himself for impact with the ball and trying to move the putter with enough force to get the ball going. Second, there are no consequences to a practice stroke. You don't have to worry about missing it, or how the stroke looks doing it. The core of what we're trying to do is get you to substitute the program you use to make a practice swing for the one that's got the yip in it.

This might be more information than you probably need, but here's what we think is happening: The cerebellum, at the back of the brain, is responsible for controlling movements. For you to perform a particular movement, you have to have a "picture" of what you want to do. Those pictures are stored in a different part of the brain, in the front. With a practice stroke, there's no result, so the movement isn't stored in the front of the brain. When you have the yips, what's stored is the yip stroke. That's why you see a player with the yips make a practice swing that looks great, and then, when you put a ball there, the yip comes out with a vengeance. The player with the yips accesses his "program" and gets a "feed-forward" of what he wants to do, but the feedback he's getting from the brain is flawed.

The idea behind the drills you're going to hear about is to get you to store successful strokes in the front of the brain, so the cerebellum can access the "clean program."

In our initial round of tests and drills, the goal is to get you to make some yip-free putting "strokes" with different weighted balls, and even different types of "putters." One of the most effective ways to cure a player with a light case of the yips is to simply hand him a sand wedge. You might be scratching your head at that one, but bear with me for a second. When I ask you to take your wedge over to the practice green and hit ten or twenty putts with it, you've got to go through an entirely different thought process with that club than you do with a putter. First of all, it's a heck of a lot harder to putt with a sand wedge than it is with a putter. Instead of hitting it on a flat face, you have to catch the leading edge of the wedge on the equator of the ball to get it to roll. Most likely, you're going to scuff a few of them before you get the hang of it. But it doesn't matter if you're a tour player or a 20-handicap. Once you've hit a dozen putts that way, you get the hang of it, and the ball starts rolling pretty good.

What you've done is essentially rebooted your mental computer. Instead of going through your normal process to hit a putt (with your putter), you're focusing on different skills, you have a different expectation of success, and you're even using some different muscles. All of those things are critical to short-circuiting the yip in your putting stroke. We've had tremendous success when players who yip try this drill. Virtually all of them can make a putting stroke with the wedge without a yip, and they use that as a stepping-stone to getting rid of the yips when putting with a real putter. Let me qualify that by saying that light yippers can take what they learn from this drill and move back to the putter and make a stroke with that club that doesn't have a yip in it, while heavy yippers need to use this drill in conjunction with others we're going to describe here. Regardless, when you start out with this drill and get the sense that you can make a small putting stroke without feeling the tremors in your hands, it really reinforces the idea that you can definitely get better. It gives you hope. I've had players joke that they just want to go out and play using the wedge as a putter. That gives you an idea of how desperate the situation can be when it comes to the yips.

You're going to sense themes to groups of these drills, and that's intentional. Once you peg something that works for you, you want to try a variety of drills in the same family to get a breadth of different feels. You're trying to give your brain a variety of ways to go around the yip "program." We've discovered that players who suffer from the yips are susceptible to having them return if they don't continue to focus on a treatment program and practice drills or exercises that alleviate the problem. The more weapons you have at your disposal in terms of getting around the yip program, the more likely you are to be successful over the long term.

After a player putts with a wedge for thirty or forty minutes, the next step is to try some funny things with the putter. Actually, these exercises are great even for players who don't have the yips, because they stretch your creativity and hand-eye coordination. First, I'll ask you to take your putter and turn it around so that the toe is facing the ball, and hit some putts that way. Just like with the wedge, you're going to send a few off at crazy angles (actually more, because it's a lot harder to hit that little spot right on the toe). But it's like learning how to play a new video game or solve one of those brain-teaser snow-globe games where the foam ball has to float into the right hole. You're activating a whole new part of the brain. The same is true for flipping the putter around backward and using the back edge of it. Because your expectation level goes down, you start to focus on the motion of catching the ball cleanly with the edge of the putter, and not on your yip.

It's interesting to watch the sequence of emotions players usually go through at this point. The first reaction is to look at me funny for suggesting that they putt with a wedge or with the toe of the putter. Once they make some swings that don't have a yip, they usually get very engrossed in the process, because that hope starts to take root. Once a player makes twenty or thirty swings in a row without a yip, he gets really excited, because he can see that there is a future in his game that doesn't include the yips.

I keep a selection of left-handed putters in my studio as well, because sometimes the simple act of hitting putts the opposite way resets the computer. It works great for light and heavy yippers alike, because the light yippers get some good training and are able to go back to their regular putters, while heavy yippers get a feel for something that could be a practical option. I've had students decide that the amount of work it would take to rehabilitate their right-handed stroke was too much to go through, so they simply turned around and putted lefty. Without any yip. It takes some time to get used to, for sure, but it's sometimes easier to learn a new routine than break down an old one and build it back up.

A variation on the different tool theme is to ask a player to hit some practice putts using different kinds and weights of balls. This is a great exercise to confuse the motor programs of a yipper. You've gotten used to hitting a ball that weighs 45.93 grams. We give you a racquetball to putt, or maybe a ping-pong ball, or one of those cat-toy balls. Those kinds of balls are so different from what you're used to putting that you almost don't think of what you're doing as playing golf. It's like somebody gave you a ping-pong ball and asked you to toss it toward the hole and try to make it. That's not something you ever practice, but you can quickly figure out how to do it. We're going for that same idea with a drill like this. You give up on the idea of an outcome—using a standard putting stroke to try to make the ball go in the hole—and just start thinking about making your standard stroke. What the ball does after that doesn't really matter, because your brain knows that it isn't going to encounter something like that in real life on the course.

Another trick we use involves specially weighted golf balls. We have some that look completely normal, but are way heavier or way lighter than standard. I mix them up with regular golf balls, and then feed them to you to putt at a hole five feet away. You hit putt after putt, and pretty soon you don't know what kind of ball is coming. It takes a lot of the "anticipation of impact" yip out of the stroke, because the feel of impact is so different from the heavy ball to the standard one down to the light one.

The next set of drills advances the theme of disconnecting from impact and results and focusing more on the stroke itself. You use another person to help you trick yourself into making a yip-free stroke. I like these drills as a teacher because I can control the environment, help the player fix his yip, and also get a close look at his mechanics.

In the first drill, you need another person to crouch directly in front of you as you set up to hit a putt. Your job is to simply make strokes at the ball in front of you. The person in front of you focuses his attention on your hands, and when they come through impact to the point where you don't have time to stop your stroke in reaction to what's going on with the ball—basically, when they get to the middle of your right thigh—the person crouching in front of you randomly leaves the ball in place or pulls it away. We've found that after about fifteen swings of the putter, the brain gives up trying to figure out if the ball will be there or not. Once you realize that the ball may or may not be there, you quit thinking about the result of the putt and focus only on the motion. At this point, it's as if it were a practice stroke with no ball present, and the yipper quits yipping even when the ball is actually left in place and struck. As a result, the yipper "relearns" to hit the ball without a yip. The next level of this drill involves the crouching person dropping the ball from above, in a random sequence. You can wait even later in the stroke to drop the ball, as opposed to pulling it away. In both of these drills, every time the person with the yips hits the ball with no yip in his stroke, he's starting to rebuild a program in his head that doesn't include the yip.

If a player is really conscious of impact and has a late yip, I'll often crouch in front and hold the ball firmly in place from the back, then ask the player to make a regular putting stroke. When the ball doesn't move at impact, the player's yip "program" seems to overload. The yip comes from anticipating having to use force to move the ball. When that force doesn't work, the yip usually recedes.

We've talked a lot about short-circuiting the yips when it comes to anticipating impact or trying to push the ball as if it were an obstacle. The last set of drills has more to do with the stroke itself, and how you can work on the path of your putter to defuse the yips. You heard in the last chapter how two specific mechanical flaws—taking the putter outside the target line on the backswing, and taking an abbreviated backswing and an exaggerated follow-through—can lead to the yips. These drills help you correct those problems, whether you've got the yips or not.

I've used the first drill for years with players who aren't making solid contact in the center of the putterface. It turns out that it also works great for players who are struggling with the yips. It doesn't matter if you're trying to swing the putter on an arc or trying to take it straight back and straight through. At impact, you need the putter to be hitting the ball squarely, with the ball coming off the sweet spot on the putter. A good putter makes a swing that sends the club on a path to do this automatically. If you have issues with your setup (being too far from the ball so that you're reaching for it, or setting up with the ball too far up or too far back in your stance), you're going to struggle making solid contact consistently. The yips only make that problem worse.

With this drill, I get you into a neutral setup with good ball position—the putter in the center of your stance and the ball just ahead of center—and make a gate with tees so that your putter has to come back on a good path. Otherwise, you'll clank it off one of the tees. To build the gate, set your putter on the ground and place one tee just in front of the toe and another just behind the heel. Then, hit practice putts so that the putter glides through this gate. You'll find that it's almost impossible to get the putter through the gate if you take it back outside the target line, or if you manipulate it with the hands on the way through. The gate helps correct you into taking a smooth, direct path through the ball. I like to actually hit practice putts with this drill, but it works almost as well if you just swing the putter with no ball in place. You can even do it inside during the winter. Just put two relatively sturdy obstacles in front and behind the putter and hit putts on the carpet. You even get the added benefit of hitting putts without a "golf" target—another positive for players with the yips.

If a player has the acceleration yips in putting, I can almost guarantee that they take a relatively short backswing, then jerk the putter through impact into a big, big finish. It's really a hallmark of that problem. By simply sticking tees in the ground about two feet behind the ball and two feet ahead of the ball, you can practice making swings with the putter (first without a ball, and then with one) that extend as far as the first tee on the backswing and as far as the second tee on the follow-through. The visual cues seem to help players remember to use the full length of the back-swing to generate enough energy to hit the putt with a more relaxed downswing, instead of injecting a lot of extra energy into the stroke right at impact. This is also a drill that works wonderfully for players who don't have the yips, as a way to build consistency in the stroke.

My final piece advice for erasing the yips—before simply trying to go around the problem with an alternative putting style, which we'll go into in the next chapter—is to experiment with different kinds of equipment. The effects of choosing a different style of putter, or changing the grip size on the putter you already have, are probably going to be more no-ticeable for a player who has a light case of the yips. However, we have seen players show dramatic improvement just by changing the look of their putters. We've already talked about face-balanced putters and ones that have toe-hang. That's just one detail you can change. You can try a center-shafted putter, as opposed to one that is heel-shafted. You can use one with offset—the face being set back behind the shaft—or one that's significantly heavier than standard. I've had good success switching play-ers to the Heavy Putter, a new brand of putter that weighs 550 grams—almost twice what a regular putter weighs. Even switching styles of putter—from, say, a blade putter to a mallet—can be a trigger that works for some players. I've even worked with players who had success simply by changing the loft of the putter. Adding two or three degrees of loft took away the feeling of having to hit up on the ball to get it moving, and the yips went away.

The type of grip you use can also influence how your hands work. Generally speaking, the larger your grip is, the more it restricts hand action in your stroke. You don't want the grip to get so large that it prevents you from swinging the putter on an arc (if that's the kind of stroke you use), but increasing the size several points on the scale could well help you if you have a slight tremor in your hands. I have a metal, pistol-paddle, Machine-brand grip on my putter. The grip gets taller as you get closer to the end of shaft, and it fits more solidly in my hands.

Switching to a belly putter or a long putter definitely helps a player with the yips, but in a way that's different from what we've been talking about here. With a belly or long putter, a player still has his yips. He's just using a putter that keeps them from affecting the results of the stroke. The methods we've been talking about in this chapter are ones that actually help you quiet the yips. We'll talk more about "work around" solutions like the belly putter and long putter in the next chapter, when we cover alternative putting styles.

At a time when expectations were very low, and the days of good putting were few and far between, I stood over a six-foot birdie putt on the last hole with a group of buddies. This make could have meant about $18 for myself and each of my teammates in a friendly quarter Scotch game. Needless to say, the question of "How did you just do that?" from one of my teammates could sum up any questions of what had happened. Heads turned toward each other, withholding laughter, and I could do nothing but shake my head in disbelief. Not only did this horrid roll blow about three feet past the hole, but it also missed by close to ten inches . . . WIDE RIGHT!!! I knew deep down what was happening here, but it is a difficult reality to face.

As a high school and collegiate golfer, I played quite often and had no problem living up to a scratch handicap. Back in the days when I had no fear with a putter, the game was fun, and it was a challenge to go out and make six, seven, or eight birdies in a round. Once college was finished and the dream was over, however, reality set in. It was time to hit the real world and put the clubs in the garage until the weekend. Little did I know that as the clubs sat in the garage, a golf demon would come and haunt my bag at night. The only problem was, he wouldn't leave once the weekend rolled around. I would often play a round with little practice, hitting fifteen greens and struggling to break 80. I would have several putts from inside that same six-foot range that wouldn't even sniff the edge of the hole. Again, mostly wide right. Golf became so unenjoyable that I would turn down invitations to play just because I didn't want to embarrass myself. I didn't even want to deal with the game that had given me so much excitement and satisfaction over the years. I was about to call it quits and pick up a tennis racket. Try something new. A new way to exercise with new challenges sounded like the solution. Then I played less and thought more. I couldn't let this mind-tangling demon get the best of me. It was the nuisance we all know as "The Yips."

I tend to use the phrase "nerve problem." It sounds more like something that might happen to a human. A problem that has a cure rather than a noise a mouse would make while getting his nose snapped while bidding for his last piece of cheese in a trap. I will attempt to describe what happened both physically and mentally when this incident took place. Even though the expectations to shoot low scores were very low, a poor round usually meant bad ball striking—something that occurs very often to every golfer if they don't practice. Although nobody likes to admit they have a "nerve problem," it is very common with many golfers. In my case, it began physically. The less I practiced, the less focused I became on certain parts of my game, putting being one of them. I first started missing putts that I usually could make left-handed. Then I became very aware of the missed putts on a consistent basis. It then turned into, "I need to start making these!" As the internal pressure mounted, so did the effort to "not miss!!!!" After putt after putt after putt would not touch the hole, I realized I had a severe mental block that had developed into a "nerve problem." In my case, I believe it was a matter of wear and tear on the nerves that finally gave way to the "object" rather than staying focused on the stroke.

By the "object," I am referring to the ball itself. When you practice and know what you are practicing, you are focused on the proper technique or way that you're trying to manipulate your stroke. The lack of practice had caused me to lose focus on my stroke. This developed into "hitting" the ball to make putts rather than making a good stroke to produce a good roll. Once you start hitting, you are relying on timing with the hands through impact, which can develop into active nerves. I now knew something needed to be done to continue to play this game that had given me so much. I think overcoming the mental block became much easier once I regained focus of the physical parts of the stroke. In other words, once I started focusing on making a proper stroke, which in turn produced the roll I was looking for. It was easy for me to tell myself I could get past this nerve dilemma. It didn't take much for me to see the results. A beautiful end-over-end roll, with every five-footer looking like it was going to pour right into the middle. Every now and again, the mind has a tendency to get a little tired, which will make it difficult to maintain its focus. When this happens, I know it's time for a rest, because I can feel that dreaded "nerve problem" creep into a nice run of ten or fifteen putts.

Now the secret! What is a proper stroke? Or what did I focus on and how did I maintain that focus? Very simple: a certain set of drills that forced me to think "stroke," not "object." The root of my problem was "hitting" the "object." I nagged my friend Marius Filmalter, whom I knew was helping people fix this problem. He gave me some ideas to try to keep me focused on what my stroke was. I had worked into a practice schedule several drills that could be helpful for calming both the mind and the nerves while making a stroke.

The most common thing I do is putt with a sand wedge. Believe it or not, this works! If you can hit putts with a sand wedge on the equator of the ball, you won't ever feel such a pure roll of the ball, not even with your putter. If your mind is focused on making a smooth stroke to get the ball rolling, you've already conquered part of the problem. You're not thinking about the object, because your mind knows that any type of nerve movement at the ball and you won't be able to get it rolling. It's almost like unadded subconscious pressure. Your body automatically knows what it has to do.

Another very popular drill for me is to putt with a friend. As you set up, have him put his finger on your ball. Make your stroke and just before impact, have him randomly move the ball from your line of the putter. Every second or third stroke, have him leave the ball there so you hit it. It's the old "let the ball get in the way of the stroke theory." Have him mix it up so you don't know if you are going to hit the ball or not. This again allows your mind to focus on the stroke rather than the object. There is only the mystery of, "Is the ball going to be there or not." This way, there is no possible way to be focused on the "hit."

The last thing I do to develop a stroke without focusing on the ball is to putt with my eyes closed. This may be difficult for higher-handicap golfers, but it is worth a try. The purpose is to completely forget about the ball. The mind knows the ball is there but since it cannot see it, it doesn't know when impact will take place. Therefore, it stays focused on the stroke rather than the object. If you choose to do this drill, you want to stay relatively close to the hole, say four or five feet. You are trying to get back the smooth flow of the stroke from start to finish without a tremendous amount of acceleration.

Over the past months, a consistent diet of these drills has allowed me to start enjoying the game more like the old days. Although each person who has these "nerve problems" will have different thoughts and feelings at impact, the cure has to start somewhere. For some, it may be attacking the mental aspect first; for others, it will be the physical part. Regardless which part needs to be assessed first, you have to believe it can be done, and it can! I know now that if I do happen to get that unbelievable day of ball striking, there is hope that I can run off a good number of birdies. Even though the dream probably ended many years ago, I can still have the round that makes me lie in bed and think a couple extra minutes at night. . . . maybe . . . just maybe! Whether the dream is over or not, I can leave my bag in the garage, close my eyes at night, and know the demon is dead!

JEFF KING
LPGA Caddie

5. ALTERNATIVE PUTTING STYLES

When I take a walk around the practice putting green here at the Golf Ranch, I'll sometimes stop and ask a player why he's using a cross-handed putting grip, a belly putter, or some other alternative putting style.

In the last year, I can count on one hand the number of people who have answered, "Because I've got the yips."

That is just fascinating to me. Far and away the biggest reason players switch to a nontraditional putting grip is the yips—whether they know it or not, and most don't. They feel a little bit of weakness during their "normal" stroke and look for something that makes that feeling of weakness go away. The problem is, most players call that a mechanical problem—"I'm just not a good putter"—and not what it is: "I have the yips."

Let's start with one basic premise here. If you're reading this chapter, you have the yips. And your yips either aren't easily treated by the drills I went over in the last chapter, or you're looking for a less involved solution to your yips situation. I don't have any problem with that. I'm in favor of anything that makes you feel better over your putts.

The goal with any alternative putting grip, stroke, or piece of equipment is to stabilize the hands and wrists during the stroke. Period. Players don't switch to the saw or the claw because it's easier to aim that way, or because the ball rolls better that way. If the yips weren't a factor, everybody would use a "conventional" putting stroke. You do it from basically the same position as your regular golf swing, which makes it the most comfortable way to putt.

Of course, that's not much consolation for a guy who has the yips. He just wants to get the ball rolling to the hole without embarrassing himself. And he's willing to hold the club just about any way you suggest to make that happen. Actually, that last part about the willingness to hold the club any way that works is a relatively new phenomenon.

In 2003, when I started working with Mark O'Meara on his putting yips, he was really resistant to the idea of using an alternative putting grip. That was true for a couple of different reasons. First, Mark has always been a good putter, and he was afraid that going out on tour with a claw grip or a saw grip would be a signal to other players that he wasn't confident in his putting stroke anymore. Second, Mark was a traditionalist. You just didn't see a lot of players trying different things with the grip. Breaking out of that traditional mold is tough, especially in a conservative sport like golf.

The best thing that could have happened to Mark was to see Vijay Singh have so much success with the belly putter in 2003. The guy won $4 million hitting it with the putter shoved into his gut, and cross-handed, too. When one of the most successful guys on tour is trying something different, it makes it a lot easier for everybody else to give it a try, too.

Sure, there have always been a few guys who did it differently. Bernhard Langer had a stretch where he locked his left arm way down the shaft of the putter and held onto the grip and the sides of his left forearm with his right hand. But that was so over-the-top strange that people thought Langer's yips were some kind of crazy exception.

Things really started to change a couple of years ago, with guys like Vijay

Singh, Mark Calcavecchia, Chris DiMarco—and then Mark O'Meara—actually being willing to go out on tour with belly putters, claw grips, and a variety of different "alternative" styles. Not only did that open the floodgates for a lot of other guys to do it at the tour level, but it made it okay for the average player to try what he saw on television every weekend.

One Sunday at the Golf Ranch, I was out on the practice green watching a student hit some putts, and I saw two players using cross-handed grips, another one with a belly putter, and a fourth using the saw. When I went inside and turned on the television, PGA Tour rookie J.B. Holmes was finishing up a big win at the Phoenix Open with his claw putting grip.

Going back just a few years, players who struggled with the yips had two major problems to overcome. First, they had to recognize the fact that they had the yips—which, as we've seen, isn't always easy. Then, once they recognized that fact, they had to deal with the stigma that went with anything "unconventional," which kept them from getting much better. There just isn't any stigma to trying something different anymore.

The only problem we have now is that teachers, as a whole, aren't recognizing the scope of the yips problem in golf. I was just as guilty of this as anybody. I've been teaching for twenty-five years, and for the first twenty of them, I might have seen two or three players with the putting yips. And that wasn't because there are somehow fewer yippers in Metro Dallas, or some reason like that. It's because I wasn't seeing what I should have been seeing. Players were coming to me and complaining about bad putting, and I was trying to fix them by fixing their mechanics. I can see now what I was missing. I did a clinic in Las Vegas recently with twenty-five players in it. Of that group, twenty-one had some kind of yip in their putting or chipping stroke. That's not just me saying it. That comes from the measurements we took with our ultrasound machine. That means a lot of players are getting well-intentioned but misguided advice from teachers right now. It's very, very frustrating to get hour after hour of lessons and not get any better. It's why players quit the game.

If teachers aren't going to start developing programs of drills like the ones we describe in this book, they need to at least be giving players guidance about alternative putting styles—what they are, how they work, and how to do them correctly. And that's what we're going to do in this chapter. If you can't—or won't—erase your yip with drills, you'll at least be able to work around them this way. Just remember that it's important to know *where* your yip is happening so you can plug that information in when you experiment with these grips. Start by hitting putts with just the right and then just the left hand. You'll quickly get a feel for where the spasm is, and how prevalent it is. Some of these grips definitely work better for a player with the yips in the right hand as opposed to the left.

A cross-handed putting grip is probably the most common alternative putting style I see, both among tour players and recreational players. The concept behind it is simple. For a right-handed player, in a conventional putting stroke, the right hand provides the power, while the left hand is more stabilizing. When a player has the yips (or when he scoops at the ball with his hands), the right wrist breaks down through impact, and either bends toward the target or spasms back and forth. With a cross-handed grip, the left hand assumes a much more dominant position, and the right hand just goes along for the ride.

To make a cross-handed grip, use the same right-hand grip you would for a conventional stroke, but move the right hand to the top of the grip. Then the left hand goes below the right—and doesn't link to the right hand like it would in a reverse overlap grip. It's still important to make sure that your left hand goes on the grip with the palm perpendicular to the target line, not rotated under or on top of the grip. You also have to be careful with your alignment. The left-hand-low setup can tend to push your right forearm lower than your left, which aims you to the right of your target. The cross-handed grip works pretty well for a player with a light case of the yips, but if you have a more severe yip, it's still going to show up with the right hand at the top of the grip.

The setup and body position for a cross-handed putting grip is identical to a standard putting setup.

In a cross-handed grip, the left and right hands sit the same way in relation to the target, but their positions are switched on the handle. The left (or front) hand takes more of a lead role in the stroke.

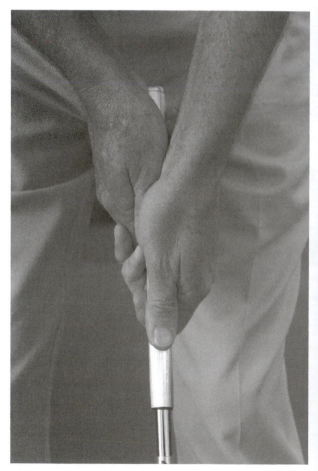

For a stronger case of the yips in the right hand, you need to get the right wrist in an even more stable position than at the other end of the grip. That's how the claw and the saw came about. In the claw, the left hand stays on the putter in a conventional grip, but the right hand turns so that the palm is parallel with the target line. You're basically holding the grip with the fingers of the right hand, almost as you would hold a pencil. Another variation of the claw is to pinch the shaft in the fingertips of the right hand, with the hand turned parallel to the target line. Turning the wrist around like that, so that the hinge is in line with the stroke, does a great job of disrupting the yip program.

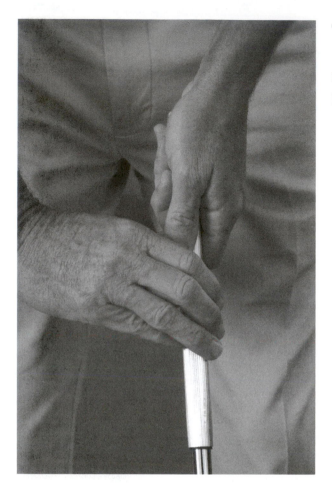

This is the version of the claw that Chris DiMarco uses—the right hand is holding the grip as if it were holding a pencil.

Notice how the right hand shifts into a position parallel to the target line.

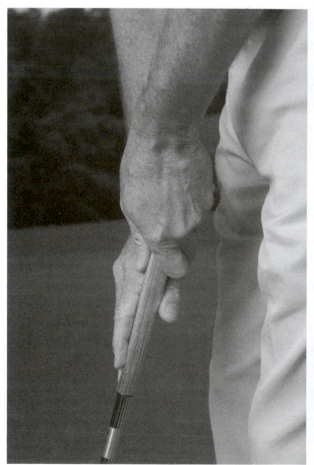

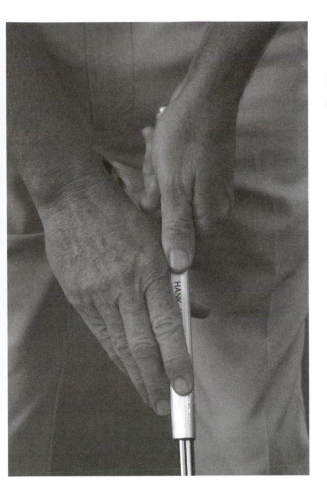

In one version of the claw, you turn your right hand and pinch the grip in the fingertips and thumb.

The difference between this claw grip and the first one is the pinching action of the fingers on the shaft.

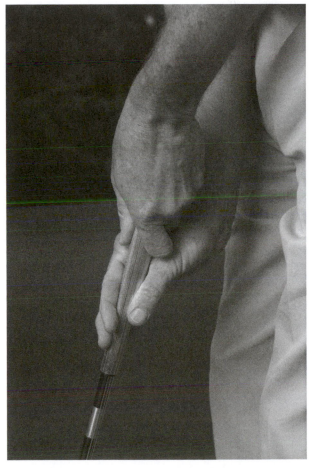

The saw grip is just an extension of the claw, and I think it's a better variation. In the saw, you extend the fingers of the right hand straight, along the target line, and anchor the grip in the crease between your thumb and the side of your hand. I really like this grip because it puts the right hand in a different position, and it also gets the arm working in a different way. The right arm slides up and down the target line, and the right wrist is really locked in place. Mark has had great success with this grip, and it's starting to become more and more popular on tour. Most of the players who try it go through the same learning curve Mark did. He was resistant at first, because it looks different than the "classic" putting grip, but for a player with a little bit of weakness or tremor in his right hand, getting that hand and wrist turned and moving along the target line feels great. Mark hit it solid that way, right away, and his putting in tournaments immediately improved.

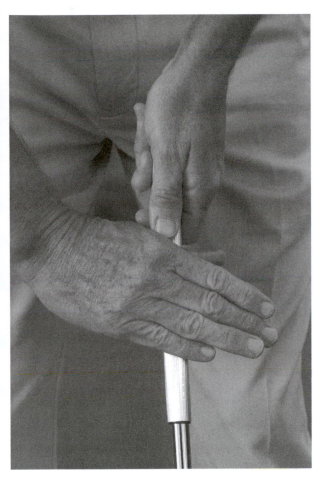

I like the way that the saw grip positions both the right hand and right arm in line with the target line.

In the saw grip, the shaft moves deep into the gap between the thumb and the side of the right hand.

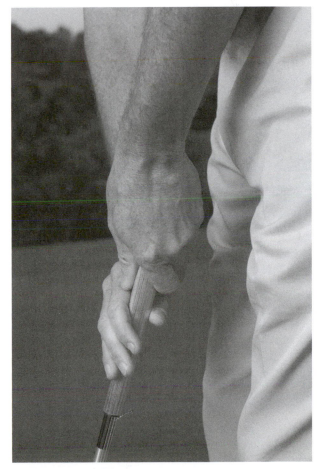

An even more stable grip is what we call the "lockdown." It's for players who have an extremely strong yip in the right hand—one that can't even be helped with the claw or the saw. To do it, you take your normal left-handed grip, and then cradle the bottom of the left hand with the palm of the right hand, threading the shaft of the putter between the middle and third fingers on your right hand. The grip restricts your right wrist from bowing out, which, as we talked about in the last chapter, is a hallmark yip position. The major drawback with the lockdown grip is that you sacrifice a lot of touch. Your fingers are what give you a sense of distance and feel in the clubhead, and when you jam the putter down into the base of the fingers like this, you lose some of that. Still, it's better than a bad yip.

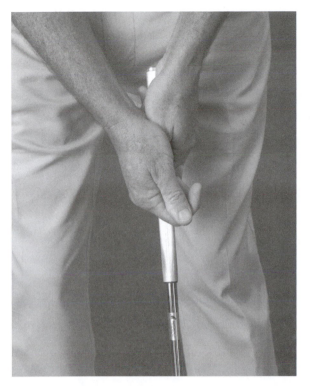

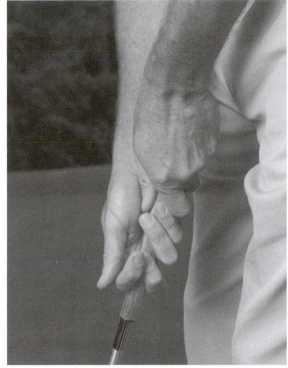

Like the claw and the saw, the lockdown grip sets the right hand at a different angle in relation to the target.

The shaft is anchored between the two middle fingers of the right hand, and the left hand acts as a stabilizer in front of the right wrist.

Another way to get a different feel is to separate the hands on the grip when you putt. This method also works cross-handed.

Probably the most drastic alternative putting style is to completely switch from right-handed to left-handed putting. If you have a serious yip in the left hand (as a right-handed player), it's probably your best alternative. I just worked with a player last weekend who had serious, serious yips in both hands—to the point that he was hitting putts forty or fifty degrees off line. We tried a variety of different things, but the thing that was easiest for him was to switch to a left-handed stroke. There are certainly challenges that go with that. You have to relearn how to aim, how to look at the ball from your stance, and how to make your stroke. But for this guy, the fact that his left-handed stroke was completely yip free was enough to fight through those other obstacles.

Changing your hands on the grip of your putter is the quickest way to get a different feel going in your stroke, but if that doesn't work, you can make an equipment change. That involves changing the kind of grip on the putter you already have, or switching to a longer-shafted putter—either a belly putter or a long putter.

Let's start with the kind of grip you have. A standard rubber putting grip is about 1.5 millimeters thick. One way to reduce the hand and wrist action in your putting stroke is to replace the standard grip with an oversize one. A variety of companies make putter grips that are two or three inches wider across than standard. They're funny to look at, but they really keep the wrists quiet during the stroke, especially if you use a version of the lockdown grip on one of them. The extended edges of the bottom of the grip are a great platform for the fingers of the right hand, and the fatter grip presses against the inside of the right wrist and offers some stability there.

Using an unconventional tool to putt with, like the edge of a sand wedge, seems to activate a different program in the brain. Almost no player we've tested with the yips has them when using a wedge.

Another way to activate a different program in the brain is to putt with the toe of the putter,

the back of the putter,

or to switch around and putt left-handed.

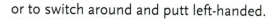

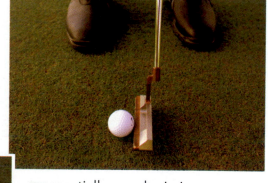

Essentially, your brain is focusing on making square contact with a much smaller effective hitting area, instead of processing the yip move.

By using different kinds and weights of balls, a player with the yips gets a different sensation at impact, which disrupts the yip program. I like to use racquet balls, ping-pong balls, and heavy golf balls.

A player with the yips tends to anticipate impact, which triggers the spasm in the hand. One way to confuse that trigger mechanism is to pull the ball away when it's too late for the player to stop his swing. After a fifteen-ball sequence, the brain gives up trying to anticipate if the ball will be there or not. By occasionally leaving the ball in place, the player also gets to see positive feedback when a yip-free stroke hits the ball.

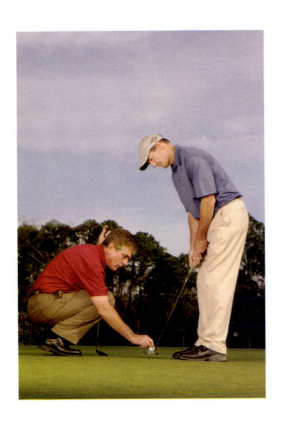

This drill works on the same principle as the roll-away drill. The goal is to remove the idea of the ball being an obstacle that needs force to be moved. Once a player gives up trying to determine whether or not the ball will be there when he strokes, the yip disappears. When the ball is dropped in front of the putter in the middle of the player's stroke, he sees positive feedback.

Another way to change the sensation of impact is to physically hold the ball while the player with the yips hits it. We think this feeling overrides the sensation of needing to move an obstacle with the stroke—in essence, resetting the mental computer.

Swinging the putter outside the target line on the backswing is a significant yips precursor. One way to improve your swing path—and work on making contact with the center of the putter face at impact— is to hit putts with tees stuck in the ground just in front of the toe and behind the heel. The tees also help you concentrate on path more than impact with the ball.

A short backswing and long follow-through is another symptom of the
yips. Place two tees in the ground approximately two feet in front and
two feet behind the ball at address, and practice swinging back and through
at a consistent length.

A less-severe alternative to a fat grip is a standard-thickness grip that is built with a pistol-grip taper on the end. The grip is narrow at the top, where the shaft extends, and the butt end of the grip gets wider. The shape of the base of the grip fits nicely in the palm of your right hand. The model I use is a pistol-type grip and is also made out of metal. The metal grip also gives you a distinctly different feel—which is step one in treating the yips.

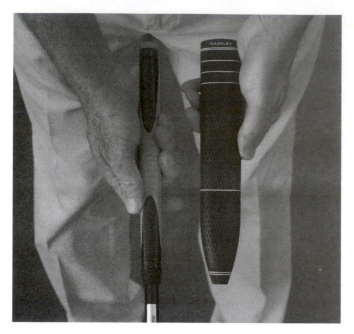

A fat putting grip works great with a version of the lockdown grip. The right hand grasps the extended edges of the bottom of the grip.

With the right hand hooking under the bottom of the fat grip, the base of the right wrist is stabilized by the side of the handle.

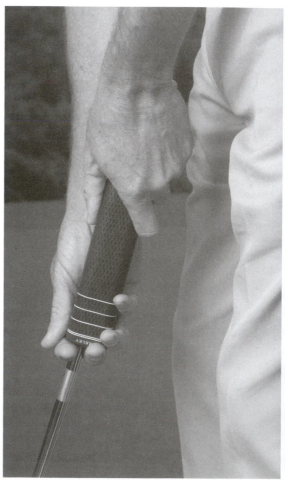

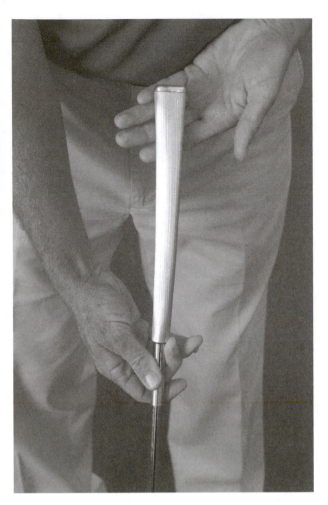

M y putter grip is a specially designed metal Machine-brand, with a wider, pistol-style taper at the end. The pistol grip helps keep my wrists quiet.

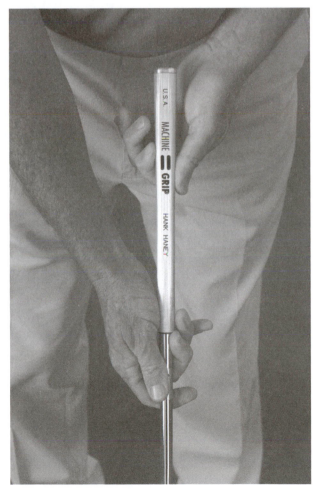

The kind of clubhead you have on your putter seems to have less of an impact on the yips, but it doesn't hurt to experiment and see what kind of reaction you have. Anything that changes the look of what you're doing can help—in other words, going from a blade putter to a mallet style. Some players we've worked with have done well by going to a putter that has more offset (the face is set back from the hosel). We've even experimented with a custom-made putter that has the face extended way out in front of the shaft, so that it changes the point in the stroke where the putter hits the ball. That's got some potential. I also really like the new line of putters from Heavy Putter, which weigh twice as much as standard putters. They force you to use the big muscles in your arms to swing the putter, and even if you have a slight yip, the mass of the heavy putterhead is harder to shake off-line.

If you decide to go away from a conventional-length putter, you've got a couple of different choices. The first is a belly putter. A normal putter runs between thirty-four and thirty-six inches long, while a belly model stretches out to forty-three inches. Instead of moving out freely in front of the body, like a conventional putter, a belly model anchors right where you think it does, in the middle of the stomach. Most players who use one keep a standard putting grip, and just take advantage of the anchored point to make a more consistent stroke. Vijay Singh has switched in and out of belly models and had a lot of success with them. The consistency of an anchor point is great, and you still feel like you're in a reasonable approximation of a golf posture, unlike what you'd do with a long putter.

Belly putters usually come in one of two grip configurations—a solid, one-piece grip, which works with a conventional grip, or a two-piece split grip, which works with a split-handed grip. When you use a split-handed grip, you have a couple of options for how you hold onto it. You can place your hands on the separate grips the same way you'd hold onto a conventional putter, just with the separation between them. If you have yips problems in both hands, you can modify the way both hands sit on the club to get some relief. I recommend a hybrid belly-putter grip—one in which the left hand is rotated so that the shaft comes out of the bottom of the hand instead of the top, and the right hand is in either the claw or the saw grip.

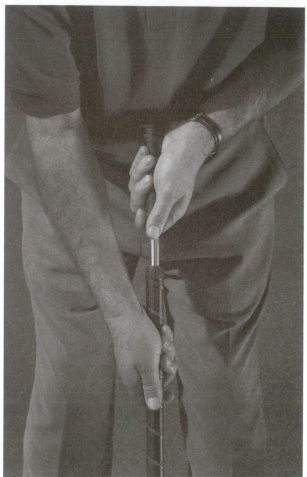

With a belly putter, you can vary the way you grip it, depending on where your yips happen. For a player with a light case of the yips, this method works, with relatively conventional right- and left-hand grips, just separated on the handle. The butt of the grip is anchored in the stomach.

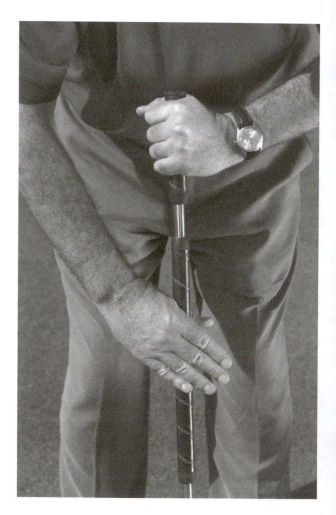

This version of the belly putter grip is great for players with yips in both hands. The left wrist is stabilized because it's turned at a different angle, and the right hand works parallel to the target line in a saw grip.

When a forty-three-inch belly putter just isn't long enough, you can move up to the full broom-handle model at forty-eight inches. Instead of anchoring in the middle of of your stomach, the long putter is anchored in the middle of your chest. You hold the top of the putter against your chest with your left hand, and use the right hand to swing the bottom of the pendulum. The big advantage of a long putter is that only the most severe yip in the right hand will disrupt the anchored long putter's arc. The disadvantage is that you lose feel on long putts. It's just harder to get your speed exactly right with such a long shaft.

You can also modify the right-hand grip you use with a long putter to calm any yips that creep into the stroke. The saw and claw grips work just fine on a long putter, and the benefits are the same as they would be on a conventional putter.

This list of alternative grips and equipment is just a compilation of the things we've had success with here at the Golf Ranch. That doesn't mean you can't try something else, like a flatter lie angle on your putter, or way more loft. What you're looking for is that different feel—the one that disrupts the yip program. Don't be afraid to experiment. I saw a player yesterday who had a grip I almost can't describe. His right hand held on to the shaft of the putter six inches below the grip, and he braced the grip itself against his forearm with the thumb of his left hand—which was the only thing actually touching the putter grip. It looked weird, but his stroke didn't have a yip, and he rolled the ball great.

I can remember the first time I yipped a putt like it was yesterday, even though it was almost thirty years ago. It was on the 18th green at my college course in Ohio, and it was about a three-footer. My college teammate and I were playing "better ball" against a few different teams of locals, and the putt was worth maybe $50 or $100, which was a substantial sum to me in those days. My putt missed badly, we lost money, and I felt terrible. I also did not quite know what had happened; I had never heard of the yips, let alone had them. The very next day, ironically, I had almost the exact same putt, with similar financial implications. I yipped it again, but somehow it miraculously went right into the hole! One gracious opponent, who had witnessed my abysmal effort the previous day, declared that he was "proud" of me for being able to "come back" and make the important putt. Even though I was very relieved the putt had gone in, I did not feel good for very long; my battle with the yips was underway.

Some background: This was 1978, I was about a 2-handicap, and had made the Division III All-America team the previous year. I was a poor ball-striker, but had a reputation as a phenomenal putter. Numerous players asserted that I was "the best putter they had ever seen." More than once, if there was a player playing with me for the first time, one of the other members of our group would nudge him ahead of time and "warn" him that he was about to witness a remarkable putting display. More often than not, I would prove his prediction correct. I remember lots of good things about my "pre-yips" days; frequently going more than a hundred holes without three-putting, never leaving anything inside ten feet short, and winning a thirty-six hole club championship final, 10 and 8, by making putts from everywhere. But most of all, I remember how much fun golf and putting were before I started to yip.

After I started to yip, I quickly became a horrific putter. My disease mostly manifested itself on short putts, sometimes ridiculously short. I bet I've missed a thousand putts or more of eighteen inches or less in my career, sometimes two or three in a row. I also had a good chance to double hit a putt from around this distance, or leave it short. I would also sometimes get the yips on a long putt, usually an uphiller, and leave, say, a forty-footer twenty feet short, or knock it off the green.

After about a year of putting like this, followed by a few years of hardly playing golf, I went down the road that many of my fellow yippers have gone down. I drastically altered my method. However, I doubt if many people in the history of golf have used as many different styles as I have. I may be forgetting some, but in the last twenty-five years I have putted in the following ways and with the following putters:

1) Sidesaddle
2) Sidesaddle, looking at the hole
3) Left-handed
4) Left-handed, with my eyes closed
5) Long putter
6) Left-handed long putter
7) Belly putter
8) Left-handed belly putter
9) Bernhard Langer's "grab the forearm" style
10) Claw grip
11) Claw grip, sidesaddle

12) "Pet" putter (a long putter that tucks under your arm)
13) Cross-handed
14) Left-handed and cross-handed

I actually became a decent putter for fairly long periods of time with some of these methods. When I putted sidesaddle, many times I putted so well that my playing companions would be trying this style after the round, on the practice green. In the 1988 U.S. Mid-Am I putted sidesaddle for most of my putts but looked at the hole inside ten or fifteen feet. I made everything. (By this time, if I putted short putts sidesaddle without looking at the hole, I would yip them almost every time). Six months after this tournament, if I tried to hit a putt while looking at the hole, I literally could not draw the putter back. The phenomenon happened quite frequently—a style would feel great for a while but eventually would stop working.

Playing golf with the yips is not a lot of fun. Usually when I was about to yip, I would know it ahead of time. Sometimes I would even know it walking up to the green, but usually I wouldn't feel it until I was standing over the ball. Many times, I even hoped a good approach shot was six or seven feet away instead of three or four, so I would be less likely to yip the putt. When my yips have been in "suppression" there is nothing I enjoy more than tournament golf. There have been several years where I have entered as many as forty or fifty events. Unfortunately, there is no worse feeling in golf than playing a tournament with a full-blown case of the yips, particularly in front of a gallery. At those times, I would rather be almost anywhere else than on the golf course.

Over the years, in my battle with the yips, I have been constantly on the lookout for a cure. Many golf authorities have weighed in on the subject and I have found a couple of them, like Dave Pelz and Butch Harmon, to be helpful. However, I can unequivocally say, in my humble opinion, that Marius Filmalter is easily the world's foremost expert on the yips. I went to see him at Hank Haney's Golf Ranch, and within a few hours, I was putting yip-free for the first time in years. He changed my posture completely, moving my weight more over my feet, squaring my shoulders and getting my eye line aligned with the target line. He also took me through the series of drills that involves randomly taking the ball away at impact. Now I'm actually using a conventional putting grip, and making short ones without any problem.

I can't tell you how great it is to enjoy golf again.

TOM HYLAND

6. FIXING THE CHIPPING YIPS

As frustrating as the putting yips are, if you're an average amateur, you've always got two options. First, you can pick the ball up. Unless you're playing with an absolute sadist, nobody is going to want to watch you four- or five-putt. Second, you can always go to a long putter. The yip doesn't go away when you use it, but the impact of it is reduced.

With the chipping yips, there's nowhere to hide.

Sure, you can try to putt from off the green every chance you get. Back in Chapter 2, Randy Smith talked about doing that for an entire trip to Scotland. But eventually your chipping yips do get exposed, no matter who you are, and the havoc they cause in your game is more destructive than the putting yips because of the variety of bad shots that can happen. I've seen players blade chips from just off the green that went forty yards over the other side. Double-hits are really common, too. Anybody who has this problem knows how frustrating it is, and how fear becomes a huge part of the short-game experience.

To be honest, we've also found that of all the kinds of yips, the chipping variety are the hardest to treat. Putting and chipping yips present different challenges than the full-swing yips, because in putting and chipping you have to be concerned with both the mechanics of the stroke and judging distance. You have to hit the ball well, and you have to hit the ball the right distance and direction, too. The fine motor skills required to perform these subtle strokes are very delicate: It takes the coordination of thirty different muscles just in the arms and wrists to hit a normal chip. In the full swing, distance judgment is pretty much taken care of by club selection, and with the driver, you're really trying to hit the ball as far as you can.

When you compare putting and chipping to each other, putting is less challenging in a few important ways. When you putt, you always have a virtually perfect lie. You're not usually standing on a significantly sloped piece of ground. There isn't any tall grass or bare dirt to deal with. You also don't have to get the ball airborne. When you hit a chip shot, the lie is a variable that changes tremendously over the course of even a single round. You might be up on top of fluffy grass on one hole and on a tight fairway lie on the next. You might have to carry one chip ten yards, and the next one fifteen yards. The basics of the putting and chipping stroke are similar, but simply adding the slight wrist hinge and shoulder turn that a good chip shot requires adds a lot of complexity, especially for a player who has the yips. Not to mention, in the end, you can use an alternative grip or a long putter to fight your putting yips. Those options just don't exist for chipping. You're on your own out there.

We've seen hundreds of players with the chipping yips here at the Golf Ranch, and virtually all of them start out with the same basic mechanical flaw. When you chip, the club needs to come back on the same plane as your arms. In other words, it shouldn't drag back inside the target line, or move outside the hands. Almost every yipper brings the club back to the inside, under the plane of the arms, on the backswing.

This move is the kiss of death in chipping. Virtually every player with the chipping yips lets the club go under and behind the plane on the backswing like this.

This causes two huge problems. First, it exposes the digging edge of the wedge to the ground. That means if you hit the chip even a little bit fat, the wedge's sole will dig into the ground, which usually results in a chip that goes about three feet. The second problem is that because the club isn't on plane, you'll bottom out behind the ball unless you compensate by somehow flipping your hands at the ball. It takes only a few stubbed chips, and all of a sudden you're lifting your upper body through impact and blading them across the green.

When you hit a chip, you want the sole of your wedge to skid along the top of the grass.

If you lift up during the shot, you expose the leading edge of the club to the ball. That's how you blade one over the green.

Fundamentally, taking the club back inside and under the plane that your arms are on keeps you from turning your shoulders on the backswing. Then, the only way to generate enough energy to hit the chip is to use your hands to flip the clubhead at the ball. That's inconsistent even if you don't have the yips. The good news is that sometimes I'll see a player struggling with the chipping yips, pulling the club back inside, and once I get the club back on the right plane, the tremors go away.

Before we get too far into a description of some of the other methods we've discovered for beating the chipping yips, let me give you a basic rundown on the mechanics of a good chipping stroke, so you can make sure your problems aren't stemming from some kind of swing flaw instead of the yips.

Let's start with the grip you should use. I've heard Tiger Woods talk about how he's used three or four different grips for chip shots, depending on what kind of result he was looking for—a basic interlock grip for most chips, but an overlap grip on delicate shots for more grip pressure, or a reverse-overlap putting grip for high, soft shots. A chip shot is a larger version of a putt, with a little bit of wrist hinge and shoulder turn, so it's perfectly acceptable to use your reverse-overlap putting grip to chip with. I like to use the same overlapping grip as I do for my regular shots, because I'm used to that feel when making a little bit bigger swing than a putting stroke.

 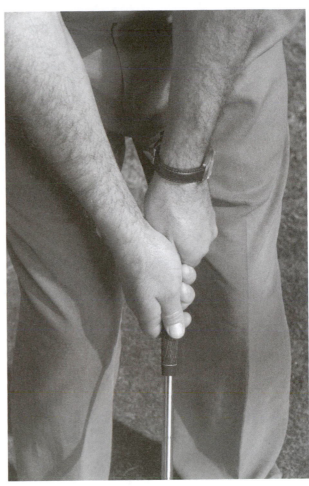

In a good chipping setup, you're aligned with your feet, knees, and hips open to the target line.

I prefer to use my standard overlapping grip for chip shots, but you can also use a reverse-overlap putting grip if it gives you better feel.

The same things apply to your chipping grip that apply to the grip you use for your putting stroke, though. You want your hands to work together, not separately, and that means setting them up so that they directly oppose each other and are perpendicular to the target line. You want to feel a lightness in your grip, too. I've seen so many players make a nice, relaxed practice swing, and then during the real shot grip it so tightly that they lose feel. They squeeze it so hard that they actually stop the club's momentum through impact. The muscles can't release the club, and then they double hit it, or lunge at it, or do something else funny to try to make up for the lack of energy.

When it comes to chipping, one of the most common areas I see average players struggle with is the setup. At one point or another, everybody has heard that you need to have some combination of your weight forward, ball position back, and stance open to the target line. All of those things are true—to a degree. But if you take that advice to an extreme, it's easy to cause yourself almost insurmountable problems before you even take the club back.

Yes, your weight should be shifted toward the target in your setup—but only slightly. You can accomplish this by simply taking your natural setup, like you would for a shot with a 7-iron, and leaning your head just slightly toward the target. Your whole upper body doesn't shift, and you aren't leaning toward the target. It's just a subtle shift. I'd say your weight is 55 percent on the target side.

Remember, the weight shift toward the target is subtle. You don't want to be leaning toward the target like this.

The next step is to preset your hips in the position you want them to be in at impact. That means opening your stance about fifteen degrees, which entails backing your front foot three or four inches away from being parallel to the target line. This also opens your hips in relation to the target line—the position they should be in when you strike the ball. Your hips, knees, and feet are all slightly open to the target, but the shoulders should stay closer to square. You don't want much movement of the lower body before impact at all.

The most misunderstood part of this whole process is ball position. Most players set up with the ball way, way too far back in the stance. Actually, I want you to set up square to the target line with the ball in the middle of your stance. Then, when you open your stance slightly, it will appear to you that the ball is further back in your stance. This is actually just an optical illusion. It's still roughly in the middle of your stance, and that's where you want it to be.

If your ball position drifts too far back, some bad things can happen. You start consciously thinking about getting the ball airborne, and that leads to a scoop move and really inconsistent contact. Your tendency is to make a reverse weight shift—moving away from the target through impact, not toward it.

Having the ball too far forward is less common, but it's still not a situation you want. Get the ball too far forward and you tend to fall into it with your upper body through impact. That makes the hands work a lot more than they should to compensate. When you lunge into the ball, you lose all your precision—your direction control suffers, and so does your distance control. The club comes in too steep, and you end up digging the leading edge into the ground. The whole idea of a golf swing is to put your body in a position to accurately strike the ball, time after time. A balanced position. A lumberjack puts his body in the right position, and then he swings the axe. That's what you're trying to do here.

When the ball position drifts too far back, you end up setting up with your hands behind the ball, like this. They need to be slightly ahead of it at address.

If you lose your posture through impact and lift up, you'll blade it.

Rocking backward through impact leads to either fat shots or bladed shots.

Another fundamental that gets lost most of the time with amateur play-ers is the concept of turning. You *do* have to make a turn in the backswing when you hit a chip shot. Many players simply freeze the upper body and make a weak arm swing at the ball. That's a sure recipe for bad chipping—and the yips. The turn you need to make for a chip shot isn't a big one, like in the full swing, but it's definitely noticeable. You want the shoulders to turn back, and the hips to follow just slightly, then the hips return through to the open position you set at address, and the shoulders follow last.

From that back ball position, the shoulders don't turn, and you have to flip your hands at the ball to scoop it up into the air. Instead of shifting your weight to the target, it stays back.

The shoulder turn is what creates the energy in a chip shot, and your goal is to save that energy for as long as you can in the downswing, until you get down to impact. You aren't doing much with the hands and wrists, just cocking them slightly on the backswing. Then, the shoulders turn back through the ball, and you let centrifugal force uncock your wrists for you through impact. Gravity is such a good helper. It's only when you actively try to do something with your hands and start jerking the club around that you run into trouble. In a great chip, it should feel like a pendulum moving back and forth at a relaxed pace. If you actually dangled a club from your fingers and let it swing like a pendulum, the amount of force coming from the club when it started to swing back toward the bottom of its arc is about what you want in terms of force when you actually hit a shot. Let gravity and the club work for you. When you hit a chip shot, the impact should feel like the club clipping the grass. You're not trying to dig the club into the turf or make any kind of divot. You're looking for smooth, gentle rhythm.

(1) On a chip shot, your weight should be slightly forward, but not to the point that you're leaning toward the target. Ball position looks back, but only because the stance is open to the target line.

(2) Notice how the shoulders have turned, along with a slight hip turn.

(3) The lower body has stayed pretty quiet—basically returning to the position it was in at address, with the hips open to the target line. The shoulders don't stop turning at impact.

(4) I like to see a nice, full finish, because it encourages the shoulders to keep turning. If they don't turn, you have to flip your hands to hit the ball.

(1) Here, you can see how the feet and hips are open, but the shoulders are more square to the target line.

(2) The club stays on the same plane as the arms in the backswing. It doesn't get sucked behind, closer to the legs.

(3) You can really see how the shoulders continue to turn through impact. This is the single element that most amateur players miss.

(4) Don't be afraid to complete the shoulder turn and finish high.

Let me say one more thing about club selection before we move on to the yips drills. I like to use the club that will carry the ball just onto the green, so that it can then roll out to the hole. I'll use anything from a 7-iron to a sand wedge to get that done. The stroke isn't any different when you use any of those clubs, but if you do have a tendency to yip, you're going to be a whole lot more nervous about using that lofted wedge. The bounce on a sand wedge is a lot less forgiving than the sole of your 7-iron. If you do worry about the yips, you can avoid some of that stress by using a lesser-lofted club.

Practicing chip shots with a low-loft club such as a 5- or 6-iron can alleviate some yip stress, because you have a greater margin for error.

Once you've worked on your chipping mechanics, if you're still feeling the yip in your stroke, it's time to work your way through the series of drills I'm going to describe here. You can break them down into two categories. In the first set, I'm going to show you how to work on the actual motion of your chipping swing. In the second set, we're going to talk more about the *feel* of the stroke itself, and then work on the thought process that goes with it.

Let's start with the stroke itself. The main themes we've been talking about here are keeping the club from moving under and behind on the backswing, making a good shoulder turn, and brushing the grass. Let's handle these issues one by one. The first step is to get an idea where the yip is in the stroke. I like to do that by asking you to hit one-handed chips, first with the right hand and then the left. If you have the chipping yips (and you're right-handed), we're most likely going to see that yip right away when you make that right-hand-only swing. When we move on to the left-only chip, you'll immediately get the feel for where the club needs to go on the backswing, because if it moves inside and under the plane, you won't be able to support it as well.

Asking a player to hit small, short chip shots, first with the right hand only and then the left hand only, accomplishes two things. First, it's a great way to diagnose that the yips actually are in a player's stroke. Second, it forces the player to understand how each arm and hand works in the chipping stroke. When you swing with one hand, the easiest way to hit the chip—with the club following the plane of the arms—is also the technically correct way to hit it.

Two other drills do a great job of getting the club and your arms linked with your body turn—not only in the right position, but in the right sequence, too. The club tends to move inside and low when the arms work by themselves in the backswing without a good supporting shoulder turn. By making ten or fifteen practice swings with the butt of your wedge anchored in your stomach and your grip down on the end of the club, near the clubhead, you can't help but make a swing that includes a good shoulder turn. And because of the anchored clubhead, you can't let the club drift down and behind you on the backswing, either.

Another great way to feel that link between the arms and body is to hold a towel under your arms as you hit chip shots. To keep the towel in place all the way through the shot, you have to make a good turn back, and then finish your turn through impact. It's especially effective for the move down through impact and into the finish, where most players have a tendency to stop turning and let the arms separate from the body. With the towel in place, your finish can't help but be great.

The yips crop into a chipping swing when you start to move the arms and wrists independent of any body turn. To get a feel for how the arms and body should work together, grip the club down on the shaft and anchor the butt end of it in the middle of your belly. Practice making swings with the club anchored in place. The anchor forces you to turn your arms and body in unison—and prevents you from taking the club back to the inside.

Another way to feel the arms and chest moving together is to hold a towel in both armpits and make practice swings while keeping it in place. The towel prevents you from making a scoop move on the downswing, and forces you to turn through impact.

If it's still difficult to get the feel for a good shoulder turn back and through after trying those drills, you can experiment with hitting your chip shots with your head already turned toward the target. Get into your normal setup position, and then look at your target—where you want the ball to land. By keeping your head turned toward the target during your swing, you have more room to turn the shoulders back without being obstructed by your chin. The turned head also makes it easier to turn the shoulders through to get into position to match where your head already is. It definitely takes some practice to hit shots this way, but it's a good change of pace if you're struggling to turn.

One way to encourage shoulder turn in a chip shot is to take your address position and look at the place you want the ball to land (1). Then, hit your chip shot with your head turned (2), all the way through the finish (3). The turned head lets the shoulders turn more freely.

You can see how a tucked head prevents the shoulders from turning so well. They actually run into the chin on the way back.

The secret to good chipping (and chipping without the yips) is to consistently find the low point of your swing—and have that low point be right at the ball. To do that, you start with the first step—brushing the grass in the same place consistently. That comes from a mixture of good technique, good tempo, and flow. Almost every player I've worked with can take a club and swing waist high with a nice turn and good tempo. It's only when you start to bend and try to factor the ground into your calculations that it starts to get a little tricky. A great drill to help with flow and finding the low spot is to start by making that waist-high swing, and then keep swinging back and forth while slowly lowering your swing until it brushes the grass. By the time you get down to the grass, you have your tempo firmly established and you make the same swing and brush the grass as you did at waist height. This is a terrific drill for both yippers and non-yippers.

I like this drill because it accomplishes a couple of different things. By starting with a waist-high swing, you develop some flow in your swing. As the swing moves closer to the ground, you keep the flow, then add a simple brush of the grass when you get to the lowest point.

The next set of drills helps you work on different feels in your chipping game. Just like with putting, varying the sensation of impact and activating different mental programs for your chip shots are the keys to beating this problem. We're trying to take the anticipation of the hit out of your stroke. To do that, we start small.

To begin, you don't even need a ball. Simply stick a tee deep in the grass, at the height you'd normally push it in to hit a 9-iron to a par-3. The tee is barely sticking up out of the grass. Now, make practice chipping swings in which your only goal is to clip the tee so that it comes out of the grass. There's no ball, so that yip anxiety shouldn't be there. You'll find that after a dozen or so swings, you get really good at clipping the tee at just the right spot, and your mind is on the stroke and the rhythm of it, not on the ball.

Concentrating on a non-ball target reduces some of the impact anxiety that is a part of the yips. Practice making chipping swings that brush the grass and knock a tee out of the ground. The goal is to move the tee, not do anything specific with the stroke.

Once you've mastered clipping the tee, we can take the next step. Now you'll actually be hitting a ball, but it won't be a golf ball. Take a soft cat toy (or even a ping-pong ball), and practice hitting some short chip shots. Focus on brushing the grass like you did with the tee, and on the different feeling of impact that comes from the softer and lighter balls. You'll also notice that those other kinds of balls don't fly anything like real ones, which means you have to hit them differently to get them to go far enough to reach the green. That's exactly what you want to do, because you're using an entirely different program to assess and hit those shots. Pick your target just like you would on a real shot, and concentrate on actually making the cat toy or ping-pong ball go where you want it to go. It's actually kind of fun—even if some of the other people around the practice green give you some strange looks.

We like to change up the feel of impact for players with light yips by having them hit soft cat toys like this one. You don't expect the cat toy to react like a golf ball, so you concentrate more on the mechanics of your chipping motion.

The next step is to graduate to real golf balls. Again, the goal is to replace the flawed yip program with the clean one that happens when you make a practice stroke. One of the ways we try to do this is to incorporate some of the more reactive elements of a sport like tennis into a golf drill. In tennis, the ball is coming over the net, and your reaction to it is almost instinctive. You see the ball, and you hit it. To get some of that feel in your chipping stroke, set up ten tees in a row, about six inches apart from each other. Leave the first seven tees empty, and place balls on the last three. Set up to the first blank tee and make a chipping stroke, brushing the grass and clipping the tee from the ground. Immediately after finishing your stroke, step up to the second tee and do the same thing. Brush each of the first seven tees out of the ground, then step up to the eighth tee and make the same swing as the first seven, but brush the ball off the tee. Do the same for the last two balls. The goal is to make the swings on the actual balls as reactive and instinctive as the swings on the tees.

Another way to try to substitute a "practice swing" program for a yip program is to set up ten tees in a row. Place balls only on the last three, and then work your way down the line, clipping each empty tee in succession, then stepping right up to chip the last three balls off the tee. This ingrains the idea that the chip motion that clips the tee isn't any different than the one that hits the ball.

You'll recognize the next couple of drills from Chapter 4, when we talked about the putting yips. They're the same, just applied to chipping. Virtually every player with the yips has no problem on practice swings, because there's no ball and no target. The problem starts when the yipper steps into the real shot and processes the idea that there *is* a ball there, and then accesses the yip program instead of a clean one. In essence, the yip is starting before the player even starts his swing. By having a friend crouch in front of you and randomly leave the ball there or pull it away (or randomly drop it in front of your club or hold onto it), you're getting your brain to give up trying to predict whether or not a real shot is actually going to happen. You don't access the yip program, because after ten or fifteen shots, there's no expectation of a result. Once that disconnect happens, you start to build a clean program again.

Have a friend crouch in front of you and randomly pull the ball away or leave it in place as you make small chipping swings. The goal is get the brain to disconnect from the idea of a result.

Dropping the ball at random intervals in front of a practice swing is another way to get the brain to access a non-yip practice program instead of the flawed yip one.

The last drill I'm going to tell you about is actually kind of fun. Just make sure you explain it to the guys on either side of you at the range before you try it. One of the common ways the yips manifest themselves in your chipping stroke is in the way you try to overcontrol the clubhead, which keeps it from releasing. To get a very graphic representation of that, hold a club in your right hand and take your normal posture. Turn back, and then pivot around and actually throw the club down the range underhanded. If the club flies off to left, it means you're overcontrolling it and hanging on too long. Practice tossing clubs until you can get them to sail straight down your target line. Just be sure to ask the other people at the range to stop hitting balls when it comes time to go down and pick up all the clubs. I don't want you to get beaned.

One way to ingrain the feel for letting the club release through impact is to actually throw a club down the range. You want the club to travel straight down the target line, not to the left, which comes from holding on too long.

As I said at the beginning of this chapter, chipping yips present their own set of difficulties to cure. It's going to be tougher to beat them than a comparable case of putting or full-swing yips, just because of the variety of shots you face in the chipping game. Still, there is hope. We've seen some of the worst cases of chipping yips you can imagine here at the Golf Ranch, and at minimum, every one of those players got significantly better by using these drills. It's a constant struggle to keep them in check, but it can certainly be done.

7. BEATING THE FULL-SWING YIPS

If you read Mark O'Meara's introduction to this book or Chapter 2, you already have a good idea of why this chapter is the closest one to me. I'm excited about the idea of helping players with the putting and chipping yips, but I have special sympathy for the people who have full-swing yips.

Now that you've heard some of the stories that players with putting and chipping yips have to tell, my driver yips tale probably isn't so surprising. The signs of the yips were there from the time I was a high school player. I can remember a specific time they started, during a casual practice round, when I was junior. Something just didn't feel right when I was hitting shots with the driver. I was never the same after that. I had a light case of the driver yips all through college—and chalked it up to just being wild. I even played competitive rounds at Tulsa with a 60-compression ball, because I figured that if my tee shots didn't go very far, they couldn't go too far off-line. I was a really good chipper and putter, and I just tried to hit it decent enough off the tee to give myself a chance.

When I got out of college and didn't play as much, I wasn't as good at working around the problem. By the early 1980s, my driving had deteriorated so badly that I thought I had a serious mechanical problem, mostly from not practicing very much. You've heard the stories about how my game sunk progressively lower. Mark wasn't exaggerating when he described that day at Pebble Beach in 1985. I'll never forget the feeling of standing on the tee with absolutely no idea of where the ball was going to go, and, worse yet, no idea why it was going to go so far off-line. I keep that feeling with me, and it stays fresh in my mind when I'm trying to help other players with the yips. I know what that ultimate frustration feels like.

As a player, I pretty much hit bottom with that Pebble Beach round. I basically quit playing after that. I didn't stop trying to fix my swing—I looked at it on video almost every day, trying to make it perfect. But my competitive career in pro-ams and PGA section events was definitely over, and I couldn't even enjoy a casual round with my friends with nobody else watching. I virtually stopped doing clinics that required me to hit driver, and I managed to get away with doing only one driver instruction story in *Golf Digest* in the first thirteen years I was on the staff there as a contributing teaching professional.

I can't tell you how strange it was to be so disconnected from that half of the game. I was spending all of my time at the golf course, teaching players at all levels and running my business. I was basically living the game, except that I couldn't enjoy it as a player. It was very, very tough.

The professional low point came in 1997, when Mark had the best year of his career. He won the Masters and then the British Open, and it was such an exciting time for both of us. I was so proud of him and the work he did to get to that level. After he won at Augusta, he planned a trip back to the course in October, when the club reopened for the year. He invited me to come and play with him for his first round since becoming champion. We'd been daydreaming about Mark winning a major championship since he and I had started working together back in 1982. It happened, and it was time to enjoy some of the payoff, and I had to tell him I couldn't play. It was one of the hardest things I've had to do. I wanted to play so badly, but I couldn't detract from his enjoyment of it by spending all of my time apologizing for pumping three or four balls off the planet off every tee. It was too much pressure, and my way-fragile game wasn't up to it.

We've been talking a lot about some of the wrong ways players go about trying to fix the yips—mostly because they don't know any better. When I was trying to fix my driver yips, I started out the same way. I asked myself every day, "What am I doing wrong?" or, "What am I doing differently?" Then I went out and hit a thousand balls to try to work it out. I eventually figured out that I needed to try something different, but it wasn't until I met Marius and the German scientists that I understood why trying the same old method would never work. One of the roots of the yips—and focal dystonia (the misfiring of neurons in the brain)—is the idea that repetitive use can sometimes cause the signals between the muscle and brain to get confused. Trying the same "program" over and over again doesn't work. It's like driving your car with a flat tire and expecting it to reinflate itself every time you turn the key in the ignition. You have to fix the problem first, and then start the car.

With the full-swing yips, the challenge is overcoming the embarrassment of what's happening to you, especially if you're a good player. People see you hit these incredibly bad shots—like the shots David Duval was missing eighty and a hundred yards off-line—and they think you're a terrible player. Ian Baker-Finch isn't a terrible player. David Duval isn't a terrible player. Seve Ballesteros isn't a terrible player. I believe these guys have the yips. And I think the problem is way more prevalent among good players than we ever thought. The stories you hear about guys losing their swings because they tried to get more distance, or struggling because they started lifting weights? If I had to bet, I'd say at least some of those situations were guys getting the full-swing yips.

The argument that this problem—especially with the driver—is more about anxiety or nervousness is a hard one for me to buy. David Duval went out and won the British Open. He shot 59 on Sunday to win the Bob Hope. He knows how to deal with pressure. Whatever his problem is with his driver now, it isn't because he's nervous. The yips might get worse under pressure, but I firmly believe they aren't the root cause. I don't want to make it seem like you can snap your fingers and make the driver yips go away. To think that could happen is just unrealistic. The only way to have peace of mind is to feel like you can get yourself out of it if it happens again. Bernhard Langer has done it with putting. No tour-caliber player has done it with full-swing yips. But I did it. And I'm convinced that somebody like David Duval can do it, too.

The way I solved my yips problem was individual to me, but *how* I did it can help you if you have that problem. Let's start with what I think are some of the precursors to the full-swing yips. From what I've seen, the genesis is developing a two-way miss off the tee because of some mechanical issue. Instead of being able to count on either hitting a decent shot or missing to either the left or the right, the player starts to spray shots in both directions. Because of this two-way miss scenario, I believe that better players are more susceptible to the full-swing yips than beginners. Better players have traditionally fought a hook—they hook it too much, then slowly bring it back to a draw or a slight fade. The player who has the full-swing yips usually starts by hooking the ball, then ends up blocking it out to the right to fix the hook. I know that's what happened to me.

Better players who are instinctive or more athletic perceive that the club is too closed, so they open it. When I see people with full-swing yips, they always have the club across the line at the top of the swing. I did when I had them, and I still have that tendency. If you go across the line, it tends to make you come at the ball from inside, and you have the tendency to hook the golf ball. So you're fighting to hold the clubface open to keep the ball from going left. The clubface oscillates back and forth, and you can never have a true release through the golf ball. That's the recipe for a directional yip.

One of the common things I see among players with the full-swing yips is the tendency to get the club across the line at the top—pointing to the right of the target. This brings a miss on both sides of the fairway into play.

I got my top-of-backswing position more in line when I made my grip change. Notice how the shaft runs more parallel with the target line here.

I can watch a good player and immediately see the shots. One is a low duck hook to the left—more than the normal low hook. You just think, wow, where did that come from? The right shot is the same way. It's not a slice. It's a push and a slice. As far to the right as you could possibly hit it. And the kicker is that you could hit five or ten of those huge blocks in a row, and all the balls will be right next to each other when you go find them. Again, that's happened to me.

Through the years, I'd seen a couple of people who had really bad yips with the putter, but you don't tend to see the worst cases because they quit golf. Before having a better understanding of the yips, I'd seen a handful of tour-caliber players who were just horrible chippers, but I had only ever heard about the putting yips. And then when I would hit the ball all over the place with my driver, I didn't know that it was something you could have, yips with the driver. I started to put it together when I heard about other sports—Steve Sax and Chuck Knoblauch having problems making the throw from the second-base hole over to first in baseball. That was when I got to thinking that it could be what I have with my driver. I saw things that were wrong in my swing, but not things that would hit a shot 200 yards off-line.

My own recovery process was a fifteen-year trial-and-error experiment. Doing the same thing over and over again didn't work, so I figured I had to try something different. Let me recap what I did. The first breakthrough was letting go of the idea that my swing had to be perfect. I stopped caring what my swing looked like and tried to figure out a way to make a swing—any kind of swing—without a yip. I started with my grip.

When I made the connection that what I had was in fact a version of the yips, it made immediate sense to start experimenting with my grip. And the grip I ended up with—the one I use to this day—is a lot different than the one I teach. In a conventional grip, the shaft works horizontally along the base of the fingers. You're trying to develop clubhead speed, and one way to get it is to have a grip that lets your wrists hinge upward on the backswing and downward through impact (not back and forth, or bowing and cupping, along the target line). I decided to set my grip in a way that would take my wrists completely out of the swing, and then go from there. I moved the handle of the club from the base of my fingers down diagonally through my palms, really anchoring it in there so my wrists didn't budge. I went out and experimented with this grip, and I hit about twenty low, weak pushes out to the right. I can't tell you how happy that made me, because every one of them came on a yip-free swing.

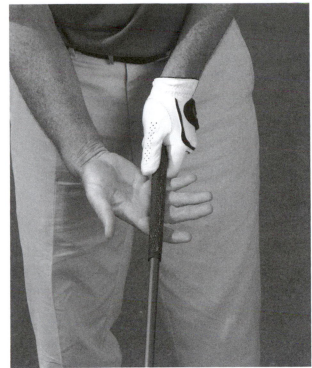

In a conventional grip, I set the shaft along the base of the fingers first in my left hand and then in my right hand. The completed grip is pretty neutral, with the back of my left hand and palm of my right hand facing the target.

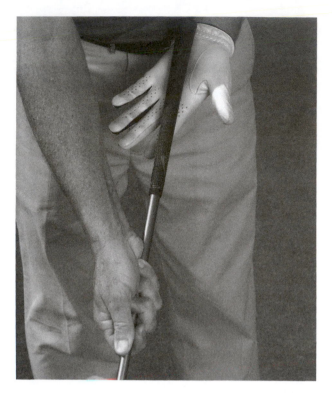

In my new grip, the shaft moves quite a bit into the palm of my left hand, and diagonally across the palm. The club also runs in my right palm, and the completed grip is definitely stronger. If you drew a line from the "V" created by my thumb and side of my right hand, it would point more at my right shoulder than at my right eye, as it would in a conventional grip.

Once I was able to make swings without a yip, I knew I could make some adjustments to get my ball flight back up and some power back. I started that process completely from scratch. I added some shoulder tilt to my address position, and moved the ball forward in my stance. I don't generate as much speed with my wrists because of the new grip, so I make a little bigger turn to compensate. My ball flight isn't back to the height it was before I got the yips, but it's close, and I've never been as accurate as I am now. It's rare for me to miss more than three or four fairways out of fourteen when I play.

I also wanted to have a whole new pre-shot routine, and a whole new mental approach to my tee shots. The mechanical changes that took my wrists out of the swing and got my ball flight back to where I wanted it were good steps toward physically hitting decent shots, but the pre-shot routine is what "rebooted" my computer and really got me over the yips. I start with a conventional-looking waggle, but then I do something that doesn't even look like a golf move. I take the club straight up in the air, to my top-of-backswing position, and I turn back and look at it to make sure my clubhead, arms, and shaft are in position. Then, I swing three feet over the ball and make sure to tilt my head to the left—the opposite of how I used to do it through impact. I literally can't hit the ball if I don't go through this routine now. It clears my head, and gets me thinking about the feel of my practice swing, right through actually hitting the ball.

In my new pre-shot routine, I start from behind the ball, right on the target line (1). I look at the ball (2), and then set up to it while looking at the target (3). I take a big waggle away from the ball (4), and then take an unconventional half–practice swing almost straight up in the air to the top (5), where I turn my head and look at my hands.

Another "trick" that's been really effective for me is to reduce the importance of the ball in my swing by, believe it or not, actually not looking at it during my downswing. After taking a last look at the ball when I'm setting up to it, I don't look at it again during my swing. When I make my downswing, my eyes are focused on the brim of my hat, not the ball. I don't get another look at the ball until I get to my tee shot, down the fairway. It's another component of trying to get the feel of my practice swing into my real swing—disconnecting from the importance of the ball being there, in the way of my swing.

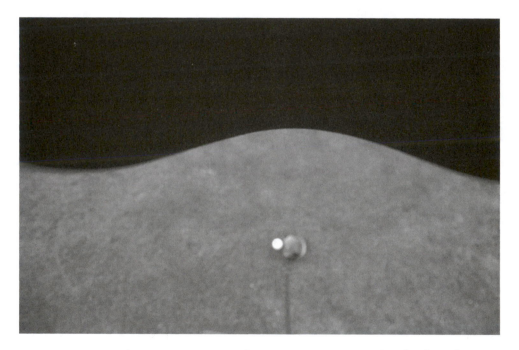

My two goals in treating my driver yips were to take the hand action out of my swing and stop being so focused on the ball. Now, through impact, I focus on the brim of my hat instead.

Now, when I hit the ball, I'm already looking down the fairway.

Like I said, copying exactly *how* I fixed my driver yips isn't necessarily going to fix your problem. Instead, to work on your full-swing yips, use the same *approach* that I did. That means starting from the beginning, from your pre-shot routine, and working out a way to accomplish the same goal—hitting the ball—but with a different process.

The hardest thing to do is to identify the problem as the yips, and not just as "struggling" with the driver. When a player misidentifies it, he usually goes out to the range and hits lots and lots of balls to try to work it out. If the case of the yips is light, you might actually be able to get away with that for a time, but your success on the driving range won't translate onto the course.

Once you actually get to the idea that you have the driver yips, you can start to make the big changes that are required to get around them. And when I say big changes, I mean big changes. A subtle change to your grip or your pre-shot routine might make you feel a little better, but you aren't going to trust a subtle change when you get on the golf course. The driver yips are a big problem, and you have to make a big correction.

You're trying to change the feel of the shot and how you think about it. You can do that three different ways. Start with the grip, because it's the easiest thing to change. Move the club around in your hands. Try to hit some shots with extremely light grip pressure. The next thing to change is where you look during your swing. I do it by looking at the visor on my hat, but you can do it by looking in front of the ball, or not looking at it at all.

The third way to do it is to change where the club is going when you swing. As I said before, most players take the club back across the line at the top. Try hitting shots with the club layed off at the top. Turn your body more on the downswing. When you do those things, it moves the bottom of your swing forward, toward the target. That changes where the hit is in your swing, and this is often enough to change the whole yip program in your head. It's all a part of the new feel you're trying to build.

We've used all kinds of other strategies to "loosen" the full-swing yips in a player's head. Making nice, slow swings left-handed for practice works really well to change up the feel. Even hitting balls with full but half-speed driver swings gives your hands a new sensation through impact. Most players with the full-swing yips describe it as a feeling of acceleration or a burst of energy right at the ball. So, obviously, you're trying to go in the opposite direction of that. The ideal is to swing the club through impact with the least amount of resistance. You want to let centrifugal force and gravity do most of the work. It's when your hands start resisting and doing their own thing that you really run into problems. Remember, you're going for the same feel as a practice swing. Those have a nice, fluid, soft flow. The club releases without any effort or manipulation. That's the goal.

Easy to say? Sure. Hard to do? Absolutely. It took me more than fifteen years to figure it out. But I've done the trial and error for you. If you keep an open mind and are willing to try some different things, you can get back to the point where you're enjoying your golf again. I can tell you from personal experience that there's nothing like the feeling of standing on the tee, looking at a long, tough, tight par-4, and then getting up there and smoking it right down the middle. Again. After making your way back from the yips. It's like starting the game all over again.

8. THE SCIENCE

In all the years I was suffering from my own problems with the driver yips—and hearing about other players' putting and chipping yips—I never heard about any real hard data on the subject. For example, what exactly happens when you yip a putt? Is it possible to measure the degree of yip? Can you use some kind of technical measure to tell the difference between a yip and something less severe, like bad technique?

It wasn't until after I solved my own driver yips that I learned that there are real answers to all of those questions. In the fall of 2003, a few months after I had my breakthrough, I was invited to speak at the European Teaching and Coaching Conference in Germany. While I was there, I saw a presentation from a team of German researchers about a device called the SuperSAM. The team, which was made up of both scientists and a talented German teaching pro, Marius Filmalter, had devised a machine that uses sound waves to measure where the putterhead moves in space and transmits that information to a computer screen in real time. In other words, the machine lets you "see" your putting stroke and any yip it might have in it.

Using the machine is pretty simple. You attach a small wand to the shaft of the putter. The wand has three small ultrasound transmitters on it, which send signals to three microphones in the base unit. Using special software installed on a laptop, the system digests the signals and translates them into visual information on the screen. For every stroke, you can see if the putterhead opened or closed through impact, the path it took, how long the backswing was in comparison to the follow-through, and several other measures.

Using this machine, Marius and his team measured the putting strokes of hundreds of players—from tour players to average amateurs. The database of those putting strokes is an incredible teaching tool. Not only does that information show—graphically—what a good putting stroke looks like, but it also shows what the various kinds of yips look like. Once you have that information, you can really zero in on drills that help the player fix his or her problem.

In the original study, Marius and his team had 180 players hit twelve-foot putts in a controlled environment, with the SuperSAM machine connected to a standard-length putter. The players in the test started by hitting five putts with their normal grip, then hit five with just the right hand, five with just the left hand, and then five with a normal grip but without a ball.

I'm not the most technical guy in the world, but the results fascinated me. The graphs offer an incredibly detailed look at what is happening to a player who yips putts. You can literally see when the yip takes over the stroke, and why the results are so unpredictable. What was even more fascinating was how many players had that problem—even if it was slight—in their stroke. I'll let you guess just what percentage of players had some kind of yip in their stroke, and tell you what the research showed a little later.

Let's start by showing what a good putting stroke looks like. The graphs in Figure 1 show the time a backswing and forward swing takes, and how much the putterhead has rotated through the stroke. The horizontal axis represents the time elapsed in milliseconds in the backswing (left graph) and the forward stroke (right graph). The vertical axis represents the alignment of the clubface, in degrees, with zero representing the intended target line. Notice how the groupings of lines are smooth and consistent. Each line represents a stroke, and on this graph, we're showing five strokes.

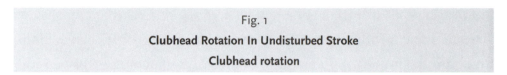

Fig. 1

Clubhead Rotation In Undisturbed Stroke

Clubhead rotation

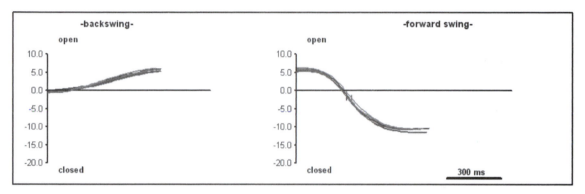

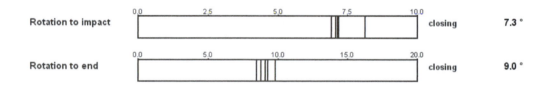

According to the data, the backstroke in the average good stroke starts at zero—meaning the club is square to the target. At the beginning of the backswing, the clubface stays square, after which it gradually opens until the rate of rotation reaches its maximum and then gradually decreases. In the forward swing, the clubface remains open then gradually closes. The rate of rotation increases gently until a constant rate is achieved and maintained through impact. And, most importantly, the strokes are consistent, time after time.

After studying hundreds of the best strokes in the world, we have found certain common denominators among the best putters in the world, and controlling the rate of clubface rotation through impact rates very high on that list. In other words, the best putters keep the rate of rotation constant through impact, without any "hit" in the stroke, or any other change in the stroke around impact. A good way to think of it is that for these players, the practice stroke looks and feels the same as the actual stroke.

Other factors that seem to play a significant role are:

1. Consistency. We have found that the best don't necessarily have the best stroke, but that theirs is repeatable and consistent.
2. Speed control. Understanding how hard to stroke the ball is a significant component of good putting.
3. Timing. We measure the relationship between the backstroke time and the time it takes from the start of the forward stroke to impact. Good putters seems to have a ratio of around 2.15. This number is the result of time of backswing divided by the time from the start of the forward stroke to impact. This number stays constant regardless of the length of the putt. The time the stroke takes remains constant, but the distance the putterhead has to travel varies. For a short putt the putterhead will travel slowly and shorter, for a long putt the putterhead will travel a lot farther and faster, because the total time elapsed for the stroke stays the same. That in turn translates into the distance the ball will roll. The tour average for TTI is 317 milliseconds (time to impact mea-

sured from the start of the forward stroke to impact), and the average backstroke time is 639 miliseconds (measured from the start of the stroke to the completion of the backstroke).

Compare the curves from Figure 1 with the ones shown here in Figure 2, which come from the average yipper.

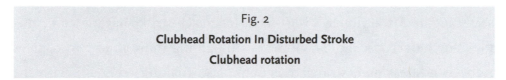

Fig. 2

Clubhead Rotation In Disturbed Stroke

Clubhead rotation

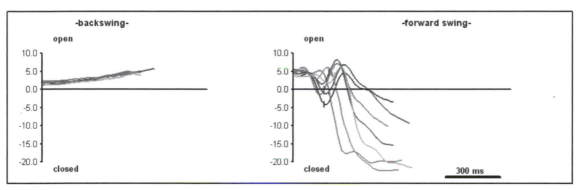

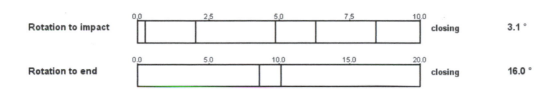

Instead of starting square, the backswing starts with the putterhead more than two degrees open. The clubface keeps opening, and the beginning of the forward stroke actually looks like it does in a normal stroke. But just before impact, the situation changes quite a bit. The clubface opens and closes without any consistency or control. The player literally has no idea where that putt is going to go. That, my friends, is what a yip looks like.

Now let's look at Figure 3, which comes from the same average yipper as in Figure 2, but this time while he is making a practice stroke without a ball. First, you need to remember from previous chapters that we have almost never found a player who yips during a practice stroke. As you can see in Figure 3, the yipper is very consistent; each stroke has the same profile and characteristics. The yipper is still aiming more than two degrees right at address and, strangely enough, also making "contact" with the same number of degrees of openness. The vertical lines on the graph indicate impact. It seems that if the yipper does not have to worry about hitting a ball toward the target, he is also two degrees open at the time of impact. In the real strokes above, the yipper unconsciously knew that he would miss right if he used the same amount of rotation as in his practice stroke, and it caused an explosion around the time of impact. It isn't necessarily accurate to say that improper alignment at address is the cause for all yippers. However, it does illustrate why most yippers do not yip during their practice stroke. And that is because the practice stroke focuses on movement rather than target.

It's important to note that the yipper can tap into a non-yip motor program in the brain, which means the putting movements are possible without a yip. This is a major breakthrough for any yipper, to know that he could perform the movements without a yip. This is also the reason why we believe that not all yippers suffer from the medical condition of focal dystonia. If that were the case, yippers would have the same problem in the practice stroke. Many yippers we have seen here at the Golf Ranch have improved their stroke tremendously just by realizing that they are not "ill," "contaminated," or "hopeless." Once the hope has been rekindled, we have been able to help them take the necessary steps to overcome the problem.

Without hope, there is no way to get to that fix. I think this explains why we have taken a different route to try to find some sort of a "cure" for the yips. Conventional teaching methods have so far failed to provide any reasonable way of treatment. The success we've had has come from trying less conventional things.

It makes me think of a story I read about a child who had polio since birth. The child's mother made a box on wheels, and she wheeled the boy around in the box wherever she went. When he got to be six years old, he tried to get out of the box and walk for himself, but his mother told him he wasn't allowed to do that. She always said to him, "You have polio, you can't walk, and you have to stay inside the box for your own good." Sometimes he would try to get out of the box when she was not around, but when she came back, she always put him back in the box. He kept trying to escape until he was nine years old, when he finally got out and was able to take some wobbly steps on his own legs. Today, you wouldn't be able to distinguish him from a person who never had polio. He walks—and runs—normally, all because he finally got out of the box.

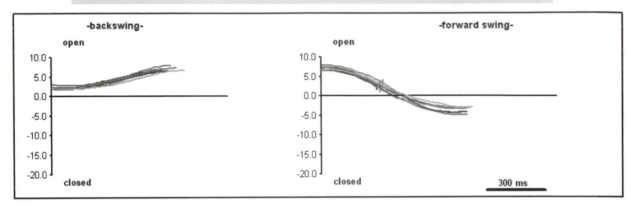

Fig. 3

Clubhead Rotation In Practice Stroke of a Yipper

Clubhead rotation

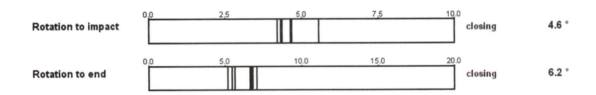

We've put hundreds and hundreds of players on the SuperSAM at the Golf Ranch. It just reinforces what Marius and his team discovered when they did the initial study. The machine tells us that something in the neighborhood of 20 percent of all players have some kind of directional yip in their putting strokes. Just think about that for a second. Now, it doesn't mean that every one of that 20 percent has the yips to the degree that he or she can't play golf. But having that yip means putting won't be as straightforward as it can be. And the frustration that comes from missing makeable putts could be the result of a misdiagnosis. Wouldn't you want to know that you were missing putts not because you were misreading them, or because your stroke was bad, but because of a yip? At least you could work on the real problem.

We still haven't figured out what actually causes the yips. But this hard data seems to show a connection between the yips and a player's subconscious effort to do what he or she wants to do with the putter and what is actually happening with the setup and stroke. It seems that the best putters have the correct performance representation (imagination) and then execute the movements accordingly, and that there is very little difference, if any, between the concept and reality. This chart shows the average rotation curve of twenty-six directional yippers—the lower curve—and sixty good strokes (the upper curve). The back- and forward-stroke data of each group were merged so as to have one rotation curve for the stroke as a whole. The horizontal axis represents the completion percentage of the total stroke. The vertical axis represents the alignment of the clubface, with zero being the intended target line.

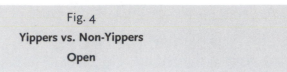

Fig. 4
Yippers vs. Non-Yippers
Open

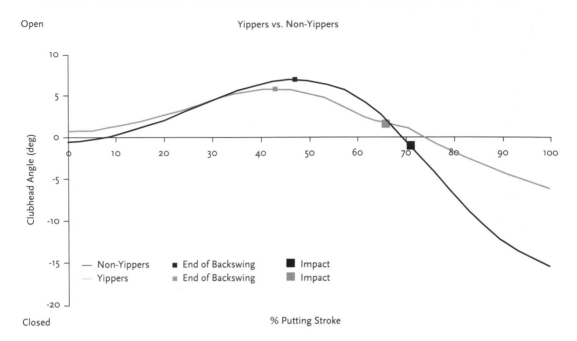

What's happening here is that players who have a yip seem to actively resist rotation of the putterhead during the stroke. You can see it in the lighter line, which flattens out dramatically before and just after impact. Yippers virtually stop rotating the putterhead just before impact. The putterhead releases in two ways:

1. **Directional: The toe of the putterhead overtakes the heel through the impact zone, the rate staying constant.** The rate of rotation is dictated by the rotation of the shoulders, and is also

determined by the position of the elbows (bowed out elbows = less rotation).

2. **Acceleration: The speed and mass of the putterhead transfers energy into the ball.** There's no holding onto the stroke. We have found that good putters have maximum speed in the stroke just before impact. Poor putters are still speeding the club up through impact, while yippers have almost twice as much acceleration *after* impact as good players do. That's losing control of the acceleration release of the putter.

Think about this for a second. You know how to tie your shoes. You've known how to do this since you were a little kid. But if you had to think about every little movement it took to tie your shoes, it would get a lot more complicated to do it, and you wouldn't be able to do it very fast. A player with the yips is trying to take control of the clubhead in a way that a good putter doesn't even think about.

We've also found that players who don't have the yips hit the ball more left of the target than they aim, while players with the yips do the opposite. They hit the ball more right than they aim, because the putterhead is held open. Players with the yips also rotate the putter much less than non-yippers, both during the backswing and forward swing, and yippers also have a much quicker backswing.

When you think about players who have the yips, you usually come up with the image of somebody in his forties or fifties who has a lot of playing experience. The data seems to support that idea. Among the players the research team has tested, the average age of a player with yips was forty-three, while that of players without the yips was thirty-nine. The lower a player's handicap was—and the more years he or she played the game—the more likely he or she was to have the yips. Lower-handicap players also seem to have more problems with directional control. And men and women were equally likely to have the problem.

As I've said before, we're still in the beginning stages of this research. We've made some huge strides, and have helped a lot of people, but I'm looking forward to the next round of study, so we can get even more precise in the way we treat this problem. In the next chapter, I'll tell you a little bit about some of the things we're looking into when it comes to the future of yips study.

Ernst Pöeppel is a brain scientist. He is chair of the Institute of Medical Psychology and of the Human Science Center, both at Munich University in Germany. Dr. Pöeppel is also guest professor at Peking University in China, and runs research projects in Tokyo, St. Petersburg, and Warsaw that promote interdisciplinary and international activities. Previously, he was director of a national research center in Germany for brain science, and in earlier years he was affiliated with MIT's Department of Psychology and Brain Science and the Neuroscience Research Program. He has published many books, including *Mindworks: Time and Conscious Experience,* and has written more than 300 scientific papers. He is an expert in the time control of brain processes and visual perception. Dr. Pöeppel pioneered the study of the phenomenon "blindsight," which implies that we can see a lot without noticing it consciously. He has taught sports medicine, linking his expertise from brain science with the challenges in different sports such as soccer, tennis, and golf. As a younger person he ran track and field, and as a professor he played a lot of squash—challenging his students to beat him, which actually never happened. At sixty-five years of age, he now owns the flattest learning curve in golf, reaching a stable double-bogey skill level after many years.

PUTTING IS IMPOSSIBLE BY PROF. DR. ERNST PÖEPPEL

If one wants to understand something like putting, it sometimes makes sense to start from a position that at first sight may sound outrageous or at least strange. But taking this kind of outside position has one advantage: It opens the mind to new ideas, and allows a person to get rid of some typical prejudices. Putting looks extremely simple, and because it looks simple, a prejudice of simplicity develops and the complexity of efficient action is underestimated. It is my experience that the challenge of the complexity of putting is not appreciated by every golfer, and not by every golf pro (with someone like Marius Filmalter being a notable exception). There is a lot of knowledge out there that can be applied to improve performance. But before developing new "therapies" for the yips, it is necessary to expand the view to start with the idea that "putting is possible."

Let me sketch just a few ideas. During putting, the movement is controlled continuously by certain brain areas (the basal ganglia). By definition, this continuous control makes the movement more vulnerable, because other influences may interfere. For continuously controlled movements (or, physiologically speaking, "ramp movements") it is of course desirable that at any instant a specific movement can be altered by new information. This is our evolutionary heritage, and we successfully use these kind of movements every day, like when we steer a car. Ramp movements are highly adaptable. But for a movement trajectory that should be smooth and consistent, like putting a golf ball, this openness and adaptability can be the source of disaster. Any influence from inside or outside may effect the movement. Such openness of movement control is not the case for ballistic movements in which the entire movement is preprogrammed, such as hitting the ball with a specific weapon for a desired distance of, say, 120 yards. (The different weapons are chosen to allow the enrollment of the ballistic movement without any necessary control during the movement). Thus, from the brain's point of view, putting has nothing to do with hitting the ball with the driver or any iron, and the challenge of creating a smooth movement with a specific acceleration and peak velocity close to the point of impact is rather unphysiological. Basically, it is an impossible movement (or if I have convinced the reader, a very difficult movement).

Because of the openness of the neuronal program during a putt, other effects can easily interfere. Depending on the situation, the activation level of a player is different; with higher activation triggered by anxiety or social challenges, all movement programs in the brain are affected, usually in a negative way. There is one basic lesson to be learned from the brain sciences: There is no independence of any activity of any brain module. Such modules represent perception (what and how we see or hear), or emotional evaluation, or memory processes, or movement control, or high-level cognition such as thinking. This interdependence of all neuronal activities that are basic to consciousness is due to the high interconnectivity of the billions of brain cells. Our brain has a qualitatively different architecture than any computer (which is why one should never refer to the brain as a computer, as some researchers are doing). If the emotional frame is altered because we are annoyed, or we're thinking too intensely about our score, or we're trying to remember how to putt the ball, performance will necessarily be affected because of the openness and vulnerability of the brain machinery. Thus, don't think, don't remember, and don't evaluate—gain the moment.

What does "gain the moment" mean? It has been discovered in recent years that the brain provides operational platforms with a duration of approximately two to three seconds. This time window can also be referred to as the "subjective presence," and we can see it in many activities, such as speech, memory, decision processes, and, in particular, movement control. A putting movement with high temporal and spatial precision must be embedded within this temporal window. On this operational platform of just a few seconds, everything else has to be blended out; there is nothing else in the mind other than just "movement." What I refer to here is the concept of "embodiment," which over the last few years has become is a central issue in the brain sciences and in technological development in the U.S., Europe, and particularly Japan.

What does that mean for putting a golf ball? A putter has to become part of the body of the player, and the putter should not simply be an instrument for hitting the ball; my putter is a part of myself. A successful player no longer has an external point of view toward a putter, toward the ball, or toward the hole. Within the time window of a few seconds, within this "gain the moment," player, putter, ball, and the hole become a unity that is connected by the trajectory the ball is traveling upon. Obviously, to come to the state of successful embodiment, special training—which must be highly individualized—is necessary. In fact, everything said so far indicates that playing golf is an extremely individualized activity; everyone carries his or her own personal history in the brain, and this can affect performance. It is the challenge of the golf pro to recognize the individual frame that is more relevant for putting. However, this practice gets much less attention when a player is learning to play the game. This viewpoint also implies that when someone suffers from the yips, the reasons are very specific. There is no general yipping problem; yipping looks on the surface as though it is always the same, but to control yipping and to get rid of it, an individual analysis and personal program are necessary.

Referring to embodiment (mentally connecting the different elements into a unified element when putting), I have already indicated that a practice stroke in the traditional way may actually be disruptive. If there is no ball, the entire movement program is different; in particular there is no anticipation of the ball falling into the hole and giving feedback by the desired noise. It is no wonder that one hardly ever observes yips during practice strokes, because these strokes have nothing to do with reality. Thus, for practicing the putting stroke, new technologies have to be developed (and to the best of my knowledge, are already under way) that mimic the reality of putting. Furthermore, as we have demonstrated by some experiments in associated fields, mental training may be very useful for improving movements; again, this has to be learned on a professional level.

What should be recognized in the development of new golf technologies are features of brain processes that we as neuroscientists refer to as the "reference principle" or the "corollary discharge." The basic idea is that whenever we make a movement—in this case, whenever we putt a ball—there are two events in the brain. One program is responsible for the execution of the smooth movement. The other program is storing the movement program and allows a constant monitoring of the movement. When the movement—or better, the action—is completed, a feedback cancels the copy of the movement program. What could be the feedback in putting? It is the noise of the ball falling into the hole (which also gives psychological satisfaction). Only when the player has heard that noise is the putting stroke completed. This implies that the player should definitely not follow the ball visually, but rather should wait for the auditory feedback. This final noise is an essential element of embodiment in putting, which should get more attention.

To reach the goal of "putting is possible" requires the acceptance of many factors that contribute to the complexity of this stroke. I believe that the brain sciences provide some information that allows a better understanding of putting in general, of yipping in particular, and of creating new concepts for improvement and even therapy. I am convinced, however, that there is not one therapy for yipping for everyone, as there is no learning program for putting for everyone; because of the high complexity of the game, every player with or without yips or any other problem represents an individual cosmos.

9. FUTURE OF YIPS STUDY

The thing that strikes me over and over about the yips is the way the problem inspires stories that almost sound like confessions, or some kind of therapy session. When you combine the embarrassment of the yips, the fact that many players haven't been able to talk about the problem, and the lack of real answers for treating them, what you get is this outpouring of "war stories" when a player feels like he's finally found a sympathetic listener.

When I listen to those stories, I hear two different kinds of things. I hear about specific symptoms of a player's yips—problems that I want to try to help fix with some of the methods we've been talking about in this book. I also hear some fascinating insights about the overall subject of the yips themselves—insights that inspire all kinds of new questions. One of the cool things about working on the original *Golf Digest* articles on the yips and this book is that we opened the subject up to so many people who were struggling with something they couldn't define. We're getting so many more questions about the yips—questions that can only help us have a better idea of where to go next. I've been getting hundreds of e-mails every month since the first *Golf Digest* yips article came out in August of 2004. I was almost overwhelmed by the sympathy I got from people who understood my problem with the driver yips because they had gone through something similar. I realized how little people know about the yips, and how much they want to learn. That's the need we're trying to satisfy with this book and the research we're doing.

We're just scratching the surface when it comes to understanding, researching, and treating the yips. We're making great progress on helping people fix the problem, but every day I spend working on the yips I come up with other questions I'd love to know the answers to. I'm going to tell you about some of those questions in this chapter, and some of the ways we're going about trying to answer them.

1. Are the yips an "overuse" problem?

Plenty of medical studies have been done on what happens to both the muscles and the brain when a certain part of the body is subjected to overuse. One of the most interesting studies involved training baboons to use certain fingers to push certain buttons for certain kinds of food. Then researchers taped the baboons' fingers together, and they didn't know how to separate the idea of the two fingers performing two different kinds of actions. In the brain of the baboon, the two fingers merged into one finger, which performed the same function. This experiment seems to disprove the idea that the yips come from some kind of overuse—that using muscles in a certain way over too much time somehow changes the pattern of how the brain recognizes that muscle.

The next step is to try to figure out why and how players get the yips, if it isn't because of overuse. It's true that there seems to be a higher incidence of yips in players older than forty-five, but we've tested seven-year-olds who have the yips. We've tested complete beginners who have the yips. That seems to indicate some other cause than simply hitting a lot of putts over a long career. Maybe there are a variety of things that cause the problem, and all create a relatively consistent set of symptoms. If we can figure out the how and why, there might be a way to train people to avoid the yips in the first place.

2. Are the yips genetic?

There's no proof yet that you're more likely to get the yips if your father or mother had them. We don't have enough measurements of players from the same families to make that claim. But I'm betting that we'll eventually come up with that link. I've worked with tour players who have the yips, and then watched their sons putt and seen the same kinds of yip tendencies. I've also talked to Tiger Woods about his putting, and he's always said that his dad had the smoothest putting stroke he's ever seen. That's just anecdotal evidence, but it wouldn't surprise me at all to learn that "smoothness" or "resistance to the yips" is genetic. I think we're going to figure out that players with a certain kind of makeup are more susceptible to the problem.

3. Do certain putters have any impact on the yips?

We know that experimenting with different kinds of putters can give some players relief from the yips. But do certain putters actually *encourage* the yips for certain players? We think that with more research we'll be able to say for sure that certain putter configurations—head shape, loft, shaft position—not only don't help players with the yips, but actively promote the problem.

4. **Why do women professionals have worse putting stats than men professionals?**

By both statistical measures (birdies made, average putts per greens in regulation) and observation by teachers, women don't perform at as high a level in putting as men. Annika Sorenstam led the LPGA in putting with 1.75 putts per green in regulation in 2005. Scott Verplank led the PGA Tour with 1.65. That might not sound like a big difference, but it's almost two putts per 18 holes—and the men play on courses with greens that are a lot quicker and more undulant. Tiger Woods averaged 4.57 birdies per round in 2005. Jeong Jang led the LPGA with 3.56 per round. Some of that comes from the fact that men hit the ball longer, but the women play shorter, easier courses, too.

I've spoken with LPGA players about this, and they attribute it to the quality of the greens at the courses they play. They say the greens on the average LPGA course just aren't as good or consistent. I'm not sold on that. I've seen plenty of top LPGA players putt, and they don't seem to be able to roll the ball as consistently as the men. Is it because there isn't as much of a premium on putting in the women's professional game, so women don't practice as much? Maybe. Is it something inherent in men and women? You hear all kinds of theories—that men grow up playing ball sports and have a more developed sense of spatial relationships, or that men and women are just wired a certain way. You would think that putting would be the one skill in which you could compare men and women directly, because it's the least dependent on physical strength. In fact, it doesn't take *any* strength to putt. We'd love to do more tests to figure this one out. It could do a lot to direct specific putting instruction for men and women.

5. **What impact does stroke "feedback" have on performance and improvement?**

We know that the human brain works by cause and effect. You are presented with a situation—like a steaming hot cup of coffee. You touch it lightly and discover that the surface of the cup is too hot to hold onto. You know instinctively that the coffee is too hot to drink. Lessons like that are imprinted in your brain constantly. It's also how we learn motor skills like putting. You see how the ball reacts to a certain movement with the putter, and subconsciously this influences the movement you make.

In one famous study, researchers in England focused their attention on a group of toddlers when they were just learning how to walk. These children were put into walking rings, which helped them learn to walk quickly and without the risk of falling down. Twenty-five years later, the researchers found that all the toddlers that were in the study group had tremendous coordination problems. The problems were actually traced back to the use of the walking ring. Because the toddlers never fell, they never learned from those mistakes, which kept them from learning how to solve similar coordination problems later.

So what happens when there's either no feedback or distorted feedback when it comes to a putting stroke? Is it possible to learn? Or is it possible to create more specific exercises and drills that take advantage of that lack of feedback to "retrain" the brain? We're scratching the surface of this theory with some of the alternative ball or alternative putter drills, but there's a lot more here to explore.

6. How do you "short-circuit" conscious thought?

Think about tying your shoes. Are you consciously aware of the different fingers you use for the task, and how—exactly—they move? A bunch of studies have proven that when people actually think about the fine motor movements that have become second-nature (tying shoes, shifting a car), they take much longer to perform. In one experiment, people were challenged to tie their shoelaces using different fingers. Not only did all the people in the study struggle to tie their shoes, they had trouble tying their shoes the "old" way when the experiment was done.

The moral of this story is that most times it is unnecessary and detrimental to interfere with fine motor skills that are functioning well. Sometimes the best way to fix a putt that always misses to the right is just to aim more left, not change the putting stroke. Simple fixes are without any doubt the best solutions. Golf is a difficult game. We don't need to make things more complicated than they already are.

The trick is discovering a way to go backward. It's easy to fill the mind up with all kinds of additional conscious thoughts. It's a lot harder to erase thoughts from your head. If I tell you not to think about a fire engine, the first thing that's going to pop in your head is an image of a fire engine. One of the keys to yips training is being able to "erase" some of those conscious thoughts.

7. **What kinds of technology are going to be available to help with the yips?**

We've talked about the ultrasound machine that my German friends invented to measure the yips. The original SuperSAM machine required a powerful laptop computer and cost more than $5,000. The latest version, TOMI, is self-contained in a handheld device, with a wireless wand that connects to the shaft of your club. Teachers can buy a version of TOMI complete with analysis software for about $1,000, and players can get a more basic version for $400. Marius sells them from his Web site, www.tomi.com, if you're interested.

The ultrasound machines are great diagnostic tools—they help you see what you're actually doing with your stroke, and whether or not you're making progress with the program of drills and exercises. Just understanding what you're doing is a step in the right direction when it comes to the yips. When a player comes to McKinney to get some help with the yips, connecting him to the TOMI is one of the first things we do.

The next thing we're trying to do is come up with a device that helps people do some of the ball drills we described in Chapter 4, We've found that one of the most effective ways to treat the yips is to superimpose a practice swing "program" over a real swing "program" in the brain. I'm sure you've felt this in your regular swing: When you're away from the ball and just making a relaxed practice swing, everything feels loose and free. It's when you get over the ball that the problems start. The yips work in the same way. Virtually no player we've ever tested has had a yip in his practice stroke. It's when a ball—and an outcome—is introduced to the equation that the problems start. One way we try to confuse this yip "program" is to condition a player's mind to give up trying to predict whether or not a ball is going to be in front of the putter at impact. We do this by rolling the ball out of the way at random intervals (or by dropping it in front of the putter at random times).

The next machine fits in with this training program. The EZ-Tee will let a player do those same kinds of drills, but without the help of another person moving the ball away. The EZ-Tee is basically an automated tee that works on a timer. It can be programmed to stay in place during the entire stroke, or to sense when the putter is moving through impact and move a ball up into the path of the putter—200 milliseconds before the putter gets to the ball—too fast for you to be able to react to it.

You can use it for the full swing, chipping, and putting—either to work on the yips or simply to tee up a ball for you so you don't have to bend over. On the full swing, the EZ-Tee lets you make those relaxed practice swings with no ball to think about. Then the machine moves a ball up into the path of your swing at random intervals. You're basically hitting the ball with your practice swing.

8. What kinds of research projects on the yips are ongoing?

The Mayo Clinic is continuing to do its research on the connection between focal dystonia and the yips, and they seem to be directing their attention toward investigating a yips "spectrum"—with focal dystonia at one end and performance anxiety at the other end. They haven't done any research on quantifying the yips themselves—the people in that study were self-selected and measured on their results, not the actual movements in their strokes. The potential role of anxiety in the yips seems to be one of the avenues they're investigating now.

We think there's a great opportunity to do a medical study investigating the root causes of the yips, using the data we've collected on thousands of different players as a jumping-off point. We're looking for a university to cosponsor that project, so we can take advantage of all the research capability and access to a large pool of study subjects there. We want to compare golfers who have this problem to athletes who suffer versions of it in other sports, and to musicians and other people who get "yips" in their motor function.

In the future, if a player with the yips has a variety of different ways to approach his problem—a medical diagnosis of some sort, along with a scientific measurement of the yip itself, followed by treatment that's very specific to his kind of problem—I think we're going to see a time when almost nobody has to struggle with this over the long term.

I've been a member of the PGA of America for more than thirty-years, all of it as a teacher at Hop Meadow Country Club in Simsbury, Connecticut. I've also been playing competitive golf for more than forty years. For the first twenty-five of those years I was gung ho. I couldn't wait to get out and play as much as I could. The last fifteen, my schedule has been more limited—to mostly club events and regional tournaments. It's funny how the yips seemed to follow the same pattern in my golf life. For the first twenty-five years of my playing career, the yips never really bothered me. But over the last fifteen, they've really made me suffer. Because I wasn't playing as much golf, I wasn't able to come up with a workable way to get around them. I can't tell you how many times over the last few years the golf ball looked like a bowling ball right at impact, when I was standing over a three- or four-footer.

Just like every other player with the yips, I have tried just about everything you can try. I've putted with my eyes closed. I've looked at the cup. I've looked at my right thumb. I've looked at the putter-head. I've gone left-hand-low. I've used the belly putter and the long putter. I've held the putter more loosely, and as tight as I can hold it. The only way I could get any kind of relief was to go left-hand-low and use my big muscles to control the stroke. That is, until I attended one of Hank Haney's seminars. Hank and Marius have completely changed how I think about putting. I have a much better sense of how the mind and body blend in the putting stroke, and how to recapture the feel I used to have. When you get the yips, you give up on the idea of ever having feel on the putting green again. You're just trying to survive and not embarrass yourself. With the techniques I learned from Hank and Marius, my feel came back, and I'm enjoying myself for the first time in fifteen years.

KEN DOYLE
Hop Meadow Country Club
Simsbury, CT
No. 1 Teacher in Connecticut
Golf Digest's "America's 50 Greatest Teachers"
and "Best Teachers in Your State"

10. YIPS QUICK REFERENCE GUIDE

Your head might be spinning a little after all this talk about the yips. I spent years and years trying to figure out my problem, and I know it was a little overwhelming when I finally started to get some of the answers. I couldn't get enough of the research and data that Marius and his team were generating, and it was exciting to be able to use that information to come up with treatments that really helped people. Still, the subject of the yips is such a big one, and there hasn't been much said or written about it yet. That's so different than the rest of golf instruction, which has been analyzed almost to death, or even the rest of the game itself.

What you've certainly discovered by now is that there isn't an exact plan that works for every single player with the yips. But we've had great success working with yippers of all kinds using a pretty narrow selection of drills and exercises. That means the two biggest challenges are coming to grips with the idea that you really do have the yips, and then deciding that you're going to try to fix them instead of just suffering. Once you do those things, and have the motivation to try to get better, it's just a question of experimenting with the drills and exercises to see which ones click for you.

The purpose of this quick reference guide is to give you a summary of the things we talked about earlier in this book. For each type of yips, it covers the mechanical basics you should start with to make sure your problem isn't something other than the yips, yip tendencies and precursors, and the drills and exercises we use to treat the yips in each kind of shot. You can use it to check your progress as you make your way through the sequences of drills we talked about in the previous chapters.

I know you'll have some frustrating days as you work your way through your yips problems. I certainly had some. It isn't easy, and there is no instant fix. But if you're determined to enjoy the game again and do what it takes to get better, you'll be glad you put in the effort.

PUTTING

Mechanical Basics (grip, alignment, and posture)
- The hands need to be square to the target line at address, which means your palms need to face each other and be perpendicular to that line. If they are turned away from or toward the target, or are turned away from each other, you'll have to manipulate your hands to bring the putter back to the ball square.
- I prefer the reverse overlap grip, in which the index finger of the left hand overlaps the small finger on the right hand. Some players extend that left index finger down and across all of the right hand.
- Touch is obviously important in putting, which means your grip needs to be in your fingers, not your palms.
- Grip pressure should be as light as possible. If you grip the putter too tightly, you'll restrict it from releasing the right way.
- Your eyes and body need to be aligned with your target line to consistently hit the ball where you're aiming.

- The eye line is crucial to alignment. If you set up with one eye closer to the target line than the other, it distorts your view of the line and changes the path your putter moves on.
- The next step is to get your body aligned with your eyes. Optimally, your shoulders, hips, knees, and feet should be square to the target line. If you line up too far left or right, you have to push or pull the ball back on line with your stroke. That's how the yips get started.
- Your posture has a significant impact on your stroke. If you slump your back and shoulders, it's hard to get your arms to work smoothly in front of your body without interference. Tilt from the hips instead, so you have room to swing. You also cause problems for yourself if you shift too far forward, toward the target, or away from the target. If your weight is forward, you'll have a tendency to take the club back outside the target line—a yips precursor.

Stroke
- Two shapes of putting stroke are the most common among good players—straight back and straight through, and an arc.
- In a straight-back-and-straight-through stroke, a player keeps the putter moving back and through on the target line, with the face square to the target the entire time.
- In an arc stroke, the putter moves inside the target line on the backswing, back to the target line at impact, then inside the target line on the follow-through. The face of the putter stays square to the path for the entire stroke.

- Your setup should match the kind of stroke you use. For a straight-back-and-straight-through stroke, you need your hands to be set higher, with your elbows extended away from your body, to help the putter move on that upright, straight line. For an arc, your hands should be lower and your elbows close to your sides.
- The putter you use should also match your stroke—face-balanced for straight back and straight through, and a model with toe hang for an arcing stroke.

Yip Tendencies
- Players with a straight-back-and-straight-through stroke seem to be more vulnerable to the yips, because of the way the club opens in relation to the target line on the downswing.
- Taking the putter back outside the target line is another yip precursor, because the face must open on the way through to hit the putt on line.
- The most reliable force in nature is the force of gravity. When you try to use too much force to get the putter to move through impact, as opposed to letting most of it come from the putter simply falling back to the bottom of its pendulum swing, you run into problems with the yips.
- We've found that the yips can be in either the right hand or the left hand, or, in some cases, both.
- With ultrasound technology, we've discovered that the yips vary in intensity, and that they happen at different points in the forward swing for different players. You can have a light case of the

yips or a heavy one, and they can happen early in the downswing or very close to (or at) impact. These factors influence which kinds of drills you should use to treat the yips.

Yip Treatment
- Experiment first with hitting putts just with your right hand, and then just with your left. This will give you some feedback about which hand the yip is in and where it's happening in your stroke.
- You can break down yip drills and treatments into three categories: those that get you to make a yip-free putting "stroke" with different kinds of tools and balls; those that change the feel of impact and "trick" you into substituting a yip-free program in the brain for the yip-infected one; and those that work on the path of the stroke itself.
- Start by experimenting with different "putters" on the practice green. Virtually every player with the yips can hit yip-free putts with the leading edge of a wedge. It takes a different brain process—and even different muscles—to concentrate on hitting the equator of the ball with the edge of the wedge.
- Hitting putts with the toe end or back edge of the putter works in the same way. You disassociate from any outcome and simply try to hit the ball solidly.
- After a session hitting putts with a wedge or the back of the putter, try hitting different weights and kinds of balls—racquetballs, ping-pong balls, cat toys, or heavy golf balls. The sensation of impact is different, and you're again disassociating from a result or from a golf move.

- To substitute and incorporate the yip-free program from the practice stroke into the real stroke, set up and start making swings without a ball. Have a friend drop a ball in front of your putter at random intervals (or roll a ball in and out of the impact area). After a series of a dozen balls, your brain stops trying to predict whether or not the ball will be there, and stops sending the yip program to the hands. These kinds of drills are great for getting the feel of a yip-free stroke and then watching the ball respond.

- Path drills work to get you out of the pattern of taking the putter back to the outside or manipulating the face with your hands through impact. One drill to try is to make a gate with tees just longer than the putterhead, and practice hitting putts while making the putterhead go through the gate cleanly. You'll quickly get the feel for what kind of path it takes to make the club pass through the gate.

- A short backswing and a long follow-through are common yip symptoms, too. Practice by setting tees two feet in front of and two feet behind the ball, and then making a backswing to the first tee and following through to the second tee. The visual cues seem to help a player relax.

- Changing equipment can help the yips as well. Heavier putters, thicker grips, and belly and long putters are all things that have worked to reduce the symptoms of the yips.

CHIPPING

Mechanical Basics (grip, setup, ball-position)

- A chip is a larger version of a putting stroke, so it's okay to use a reverse overlap putting grip if you like that feel more than a standard overlapping grip.
- As with putting, lighter grip pressure is better. This is a touch-and-feel kind of shot. Tight grip pressure can keep the club from swinging through impact.
- In your setup, weight should be shifted just slightly toward the target, which you can accomplish by tilting your head slightly.
- Set up with your hips in the position you want them to be at impact—about fifteen degrees open. The hips, knees, and feet are slightly open to the target, while the shoulders are closer to square to the target line.
- Most players set up with the ball too far back in the stance. That can cause you to scoop at it to try to get the ball airborne. Ball position should actually be closer to the middle of your stance. When you set up square to the target line and then open your stance slightly, it makes the ball appear to be back in the stance. Actually, it's still in the center.

Stroke

- A chipping stroke is a larger version of a putt, with some shoulder turn and a slight wrist hinge.
- Shoulder turn is what most players struggle with. You have to make a shoulder turn on the backswing, then turn through impact.

If you don't turn the shoulders, the arms work independently of the body, and it's almost impossible to make consistent contact with the ball.

- The shoulder turn is what produces the energy in the stroke. Let gravity do most of the work on the downswing. When you add speed with the hands or wrists, you run into problems.
- A good chip stroke brushes the grass. You don't want to make a divot or dig into the ground in any way.

Yip Tendencies

- Virtually every player with the chipping yips brings the club back under the plane of the arms and behind the body on the backswing.
- This flaw causes two major problems. It exposes the digging edge of the sole of the club, so if you hit it fat, you'll lay sod over it. And when the club gets too flat like that, it also makes you bottom out behind the ball. The only way to save it is to flip your hands at the ball. Stub a few chips that way, and you're on your way to the yips.
- A less common but still problematic yips precursor is bringing the club back way outside the target line on the backswing. As in putting, this basically forces you to open the clubhead on the way through impact. Holding the club open (and preventing it from releasing) is a yip move.

Yip Treatment

- Start by hitting a few chips with just the right hand, and then just the left hand. It's a good way to start because it tells you a lot about both your chipping stroke and your yips. If you take the club back off plane, you won't be able to support it with just one hand.

- To get the feeling of the club swinging in tandem with the body, start by making some swings with your grip set down by the club-head, and the butt of the club anchored in your belly.

- Another way to get that feel is to hold a towel under your armpits and across your chest. Hit some chip shots and hold that towel in place. It forces you to maintain the linkage between your arms and chest as you turn back and through.

- Once you've worked on your plane and turn, practice getting the feel for brushing the grass and varying the sensation you get at impact. Start by practicing clipping tees from the ground, and work your way up to chipping ping-pong balls, racquetballs, and other non-golf balls. The different sensation at impact (and the fact that they don't fly like golf balls) helps you think about your stroke instead of impact or results.

- The key to moving successfully to chipping real balls again is to work on replacing the yip program with a clean one. Set up ten tees in a line, about six inches apart. Put balls on the last three. Practice clipping the seven clean tees, one after the other, and moving seamlessly to the three teed-up balls and chipping those with the same motion.

- You can also use variations of the drills we talked about in the putting chapter—having a friend randomly move the ball away or leave it in place (or randomly drop it in front of your club as you swing). The random element confuses your brain and gets you to stop anticipating impact.

FULL SWING

Mechanical Basics

- As with putting and chipping, players who struggle with the full-swing yips seem to have some common mechanical problems. One is the club crossing the line at the top—pointing right of the target, instead of parallel to the target line. Another is trying to consciously open the clubface through impact.

Yip Tendencies

- Players with full-swing yips tend to be more accomplished. The problem seems to start when a good player goes from hooking the ball to fading it, and then missing on both sides of the fairway. The two-way miss starts to breed the tendency to overcontrol the clubhead through impact.
- A good player usually has a sense of where the clubhead is during the swing. He feels like the face is shut, so his natural response is to open it. Overcontrolling the club and trying to hold it open through impact is basically the definition of a full-swing yip.
- The natural response to spraying the driver is to go out and hit tons of balls. This only makes the yip problem worse, because

you're practicing the same yip program, not a replacement program.

- Full-swing yips vary in intensity. Some players with light driver yips really notice the problem under pressure. Others with serious cases (like mine) literally cannot hit the ball with any consistent idea of where it's going.
- The irony of the driver yips is that for many players, the misses that come off the club are wild in terms of direction, but consistent in terms of pattern. I could hit five balls eighty yards off line to the right, but I would have crushed each one, and all five would be in the same general area, just two fairways over.
- Driver yips tend to be the most devastating for tour players. No tour-level player has ever come back from full-swing yips. That might change as we understand more and more about treatment, but the damage they do to a player's confidence is formidable.

Yip Treatment
- The least invasive step is to adjust your grip so that it runs much more in the palms than in the base of the fingers. I moved my grip so that the handle runs diagonally across my palm. It basically takes all the hand action out of my swing.
- If you can adjust your grip and stop feeling the yip, you can then make mechanical adjustments to get your ball flight back to normal—like moving your ball position forward, or tilting a little bit away from the target at address.
- Instead of hitting hundreds of balls the way you used to, you have to try different things with your swing. For me, that means

making a practice swing that doesn't look like a real golf move, and concentrating on finishing in a different position than I did before. I'm trying to keep the feel of my practice swing—loose and free—when I actually hit the ball.

- The less concerned about the ball you are, the better off you'll be. I actually don't even look at it when I'm hitting a shot with my driver. I focus on the brim of my visor all the way through impact. The ball is just a blurry spot in my peripheral vision.

ACKNOWLEDGMENTS

I t took twenty years of struggle with my driver yips before I figured out how to beat them. The best part about writing this book is the idea that something I have to say could help players out there who have a similar problem. This book is for you guys, because I know how much fun the game can be, and how devastating it is when that fun is taken away. I want you guys out there enjoying yourselves this summer, not out looking for some other hobby.

The book itself didn't take twenty years to put together, but it might have without the help I got from a terrific team. I work with Matt Rudy and Dom Furore on my articles for *Golf Digest,* and they did as great of a job with the words and pictures here as they do month to month in the magazine. They're are true professionals, and good friends. Marius Filmalter brought his knowledge of putting, aptitude for technology, and contacts with some of the brightest scientists in the world to this project. A whole lot of players are better putters because they've met him. Marius's assistant, Pierre Noizet, has also been a big help in the research we've been doing both on the yips in general and for this book.

I also want to thank the teachers I work with here in Dallas, and all the players I've had the chance to teach. I'm always learning new things from you.